The Great CANADIAN Cookbook

Victoria Hutton

CLB 2419
This edition published 1991 by
Whitecap Books Ltd.
1086 West 3rd Street
North Vancouver, B.C.
Canada V7P 3JS
Copyright © 1990 Colour Library Books Ltd.,
Godalming, Surrey, England.
Printed in Hong Kong by Leefung Asco Printers Ltd.
ISBN 1-895099-85-4

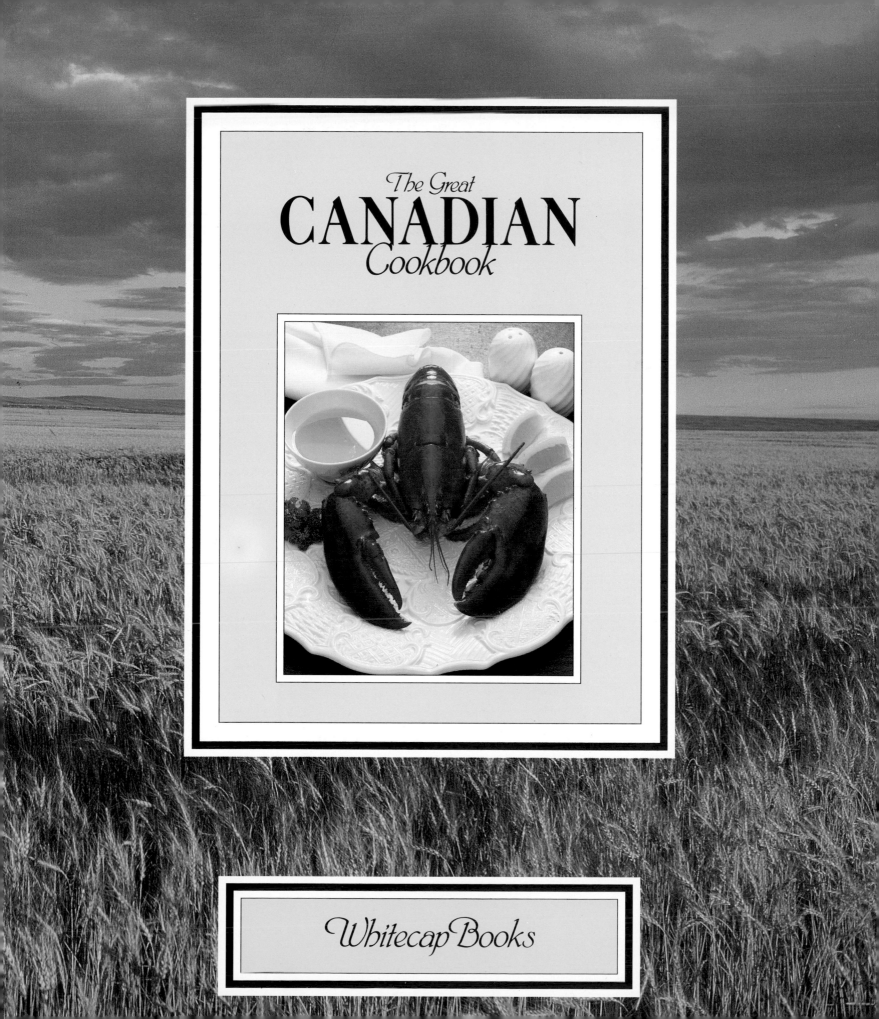

The Great
CANADIAN
Cookbook

Whitecap Books

Contents

Inset previous page: Boiled Nova Scotia Lobster.
Facing page: Rhubarb Sorbet.

Introduction

"There is great work to be done in Canadian kitchens."
...advice from *The Canadian Home Cook Book*, published in 1877, to women looking after their families in the New World.

Indeed, great work was done in Canadian kitchens in those early days of our newly Confederated country. The contribution of those trail-blazing but innovative cooks had yet to be fully celebrated. The women who nourished a nation as it struggled to settle this harsh, beautiful land could take no time for accolades ... for them there were, quite simply, mouths to feed. But before that, the livestock had to be cared for, the garden tended, the milk churned, the produce picked and often pickled, the fires in uncertain stoves to be constantly tended.

It was their origins that inspired them to cook creatively in such a challenging environment. Canadian cooks brought with them the treasured recipes, techniques and traditions of many backgrounds. Those immigrants, first from Britain, France and, as United Empire Loyalists, from America, then later from Continental Europe and the Orient, came seeking a new land, a new life and fresh opportunities.

In time, some melding of these diverse cultures and identities began to take place; but for the most part these settlers retained their ethnic and religious traditions and created the rich tapestry of Canadian culture. The enduring result was the preservation and development of a heritage of cooking skills which encompassed not only the past traditions of many lands but incorporated the growing bounty offered by the New World.

Today, our Canadian cuisine is a rich overlapping of these early influences, of the subsequent development of regional cooking styles and of a more modern abundance of natural produce. There are, of course, the dishes which derive from the natural and unique delicacies encountered in Canada – such as the Saskatoon berries of the Prairies and the tiny, tasty wild blueberries which flourish in the Maritimes; the sweet springtime syrup of the maple tree found in Ontario and Quebec, and the young curled fern fiddleheads which rise in the hidden springs of New Brunswick. Many dishes incorporating these distinctive ingredients were devised by enterprising pioneer cooks, using their ancestors' original British and American "receipts" as a basis.

Canada's diverse climate and geography have also given rise to particular species of universal ingredients that surely must be represented as truly Canadian; our sweetly cured Canadian bacon heads this list, along with the tiny, tender Malpeque oyster. The honey sweet, but sharp, tender and crisp qualities of the McIntosh Red apple has all but surpassed any other ... perhaps sharing fame with the Delicious, but nonetheless rising to world fame from its discovery in 1811 as a single tree by John McIntosh in Dundela, Ontario. The old East–West debate as to the superiority of Atlantic or Pacific salmon only subsides when a taste of either's succulent flesh confirms that the choice can only be the fish in hand! Add to that the delicacy of arctic char, the incomparable flavor of the Novia Scotia lobster, or the intense purity and richness of the Brome Lake Duckling ... and the wealth of Canada's natural food resources reawakens a chord of national pride.

This rich menu of natural resources was further influenced by the cultural "hopscotch" of the settlers' movements throughout the nineteenth and twentieth centuries, resulting in the survival and blending of many culinary styles, including Italian, Polish, Ukrainian and Greek.

The most influential of these regional cuisines is still to be found in Quebec, stirring from the old French traditions and a hearty Voyageur requirement for sustaining and heartwarming food. From this heritage grew such national dishes as Tourtiere – originally a two crusted pie filled with pigeon, now a hearty pork affair still relished at traditional French Canadian Christmas Eve celebrations. Fragrant kettles of pot-au-feu, roasts and ragouts, maple baked beans, warming pea soups, savory game terrines and crusty sugar pies ... all had their origins in simple backwoods kitchens. These dishes and many more are with us still, and although they have been lightened and refined to suit our modern lifestyles, they remain wholly Canadian in technique and natural ingredient.

Maritime cooking, influenced by the bounty of the Eastern seaboard, as well as the Scottish, Acadian and Loyalist settlements which flourished here, has come to be known as "down-home" cooking. It is characterized by a simplicity and goodness that relies on the freshest of natural ingredients. Who could not respond to the mouthwatering sight of a steaming clam chowder, brimming with sweet baby clams, tender Prince Edward Island potatoes and fresh cream? Add a basket of buttermilk biscuits fresh from the oven, a scoop of newly churned butter and a cinnamonny apple crisp waiting on the windowsill, and the home-cooked picture is complete. This is Canadian cooking as generations of Easterners have known it, and the way it continues to be.

The traditions of Mennonite cooking remain synonymous with plentiful repasts. Just a mention of Kitchener, Ontario summons up visions of markets filled with spicy sausages, baked hams and bacon; ageing cheeses and honey sweet and savory pickled produce. The Mennonites and Eastern Europeans also settled in Manitoba, Alberta and British Columbia, where the strong western wheat contributed to a tradition of home-style baking which has enriched Canada's culinary history immensely.

The fertile soils, gentle climate and lush valleys of British Columbia have all contributed to make this area Canada's land of plenty. Here the abundance of natural food products, combined with the converging influences of early British, American, Japanese and Chinese settlers created a unique and healthful regional style that has evolved over the years. More recently, innovative Californian trends based on a similarly endowed natural environment have added their influence to this naturally receptive culinary scene, and the effect has been a creative and unique emphasis on the use of local fresh fish, seafood, produce and wines in a lovely, light "west coast" style.

The current trends towards comfort foods, or those that we all remember nourishing us as youngsters, would raise a smile from our ancestral cooks. No one knew more than they the importance of good cooking in building strong bodies, healthy minds and good memories. Their long hours and hard work have resulted in a legacy of recipes which, regardless of origin, has become an integral part of the fabric of our Canadian culinary life.

Now Canada cooks ... with pleasure!

CHAPTER
1
Soups and Appetizers

SERVES 6

SPICY SHRIMP BISQUE

A piquant and robust recipe that will make a dazzling start to an important dinner. Not a smooth purée like its French counterpart, this colorful Cajun-style bisque is luscious and loaded with good flavors.

PREPARATION TIME: 20 minutes

COOKING TIME: 8-10 minutes

---

3 tbsps butter or margarine
1 onion, finely chopped
1 red pepper, seeded and finely chopped
2 sticks celery, finely chopped
1 clove garlic, minced
Pinch dry mustard and cayenne pepper

2 tsps paprika
3 tbsps flour
4 cups fish stock
1 sprig thyme and bay leaf
8oz raw, peeled shrimp
Salt and pepper
Snipped chives

Melt the butter or margarine and add the onion, pepper, celery and garlic. Cook gently to soften.

Stir in the mustard, cayenne, paprika and flour. Cook about 3 minutes over gentle heat, stirring occasionally.

Pour on the stock gradually, stirring until well blended. Add the thyme and bay leaf and bring to the boil. Reduce the heat and simmer about 5 minutes or until thickened, stirring occasionally.

Add the prawns and cook until pink and curled, about 5 minutes. Season with salt and pepper to taste and top with snipped chives before serving.

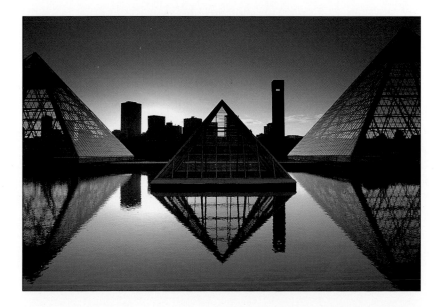

Previous pages: Heart's Content, Newfoundland. Left: Edmonton's Muttart Conservatory, where glass pyramids house plants from various different climatic zones.

Facing page: mist shrouds the sea at Sea Lion Rocks on the coast of British Columbia.

SERVES 4

AVOCADO SOUP

Naturally rich and mellow in flavor, this cool avocado soup is lightened and given a tangy touch with the addition of fresh yogurt. Perfect for easy summer entertaining.

PREPARATION TIME: 20-25 minutes plus 2 hours for the soup to chill in the refrigerator

2 large ripe avocados	Juice of 1 lemon
1½ cups natural yogurt	2 tsps chopped fresh oregano
2 cups chicken or vegetable stock	Salt and white pepper
½ clove garlic, minced	Chopped parsley to garnish

Cut the avocados in half lengthwise and twist to separate. Tap the stone sharply with a knife and twist to remove.

Place the avocado halves cut side down on a flat surface. Score the skin with a sharp knife and then peel the strips of skin backwards to remove them.

Cut the avocado into pieces and place in a food processor. Reserve 4 tbsps yogurt and add the remaining yogurt and other ingredients, except the parsley, to the avocado. Process until smooth and chill thoroughly.

Pour the soup into bowls or a tureen and garnish with reserved yogurt. Sprinkle with parsley and serve chilled.

SERVES 4

OREGANO OYSTERS

The combination of oregano and the anise taste of Pernod is an unusual but very complimentary one, especially with fresh Malpeque oysters.

PREPARATION TIME: 25 minutes

COOKING TIME: 20-25 minutes including time to cook the bacon

1 tbsp butter or margarine	¾ cup heavy cream
1 clove garlic, crushed	Salt and pepper
1 tbsp chopped parsley	24 oysters on the half shell
1 tbsp chopped fresh oregano or	12 strips bacon, cooked and
1½ tsps dried oregano	crumbled
1 tbsp Pernod	Coarse salt

Melt the butter or margarine in a saucepan. Add the garlic and cook to soften, but do not brown.

Add the parsley, oregano, Pernod and cream. Bring to the boil and lower the heat to simmering. Strain on any liquid from the oysters and then loosen them from their shells with a small, sharp knife.

Cook the mixture until reduced by about one quarter and slightly thickened. Test the seasoning and set the mixture aside.

Pour about 1 inch coarse salt into a baking pan.

Place the oysters on top of the salt and twist the shells into the salt so that they stand level.

Spoon some of the cream over each oyster and sprinkle with the crumbled bacon.

Bake in a pre-heated 400°F oven for 15-18 minutes. Serve immediately.

Peggy's Cove is one of Nova Scotia's smallest and most picturesque fishing villages.

SERVES 4-6

CORN AND POTATO CHOWDER

A warm and welcoming meal in a bowl, variations of this chowder have sustained Canadians since the early pioneer days. Using fresh sweetcorn makes it especially tasty!

PREPARATION TIME: 25 minutes

COOKING TIME: 25-30 minutes

6 medium potatoes, peeled
Chicken or vegetable stock
1 onion, finely chopped
2 tbsps butter or margarine
1 tbsp flour
4oz cooked ham or bacon, chopped

4 ears fresh corn or about 4oz
  canned or frozen corn
3 cups milk
Salt and dash tabasco
Finely chopped parsley

Quarter the potatoes and place them in a deep saucepan. Add stock to cover and the onion, and bring the mixture to the boil. Lower the heat and simmer, partially covered, until the potatoes are soft, about 15-20 minutes.

Drain the potatoes, reserving ¾ pint of the cooking liquid. Mash the potatoes and combine with reserved liquid.

Melt the butter or margarine in a clean pan, add the ham and cook briefly. Stir in the flour and pour over the potato mixture, mixing well.

If using fresh corn, remove the husks and silk and, holding one end of the corn, stand the ear upright. Use a large, sharp knife and cut against the cob vertically from top to bottom just scraping off the kernels. Add the corn and milk to the potato mixture and bring almost to the boil. Do not boil the corn rapidly as this will toughen it. Add a pinch of salt and a dash of tabasco, and garnish with parsley before serving.

SERVES 4

CHÈVRE SALAD WITH TARRAGON

Whether you use locally made fresh, or choose from the variety of imported, the tangy taste of chèvre, or goat cheese, provides a refreshing yet light start to a special meal. Accompany with a crisp, tarragon flavored salad.

PREPARATION TIME: 25 minutes

COOKING TIME: 5 minutes

12 small slices white bread	1 tbsp chopped fresh tarragon
4 small goat cheeses (not too fresh)	1 tbsp tarragon vinegar
4 small servings of mixed green salad, washed and dried	2 tbsps olive oil
	Salt and pepper

Using a pastry cutter, cut the sliced bread into 12 rounds

Cut each cheese horizontally into 3 rounds and place on the prepared bread rounds.

Sprinkle the chopped tarragon over the cheese rounds.

To prepare the dressing, mix together the tarragon vinegar, olive oil, salt and pepper. Stir or shake well and pour over the prepared mixed green salad.

Place the cheese and bread rounds into a moderately hot oven and cook until the cheese melts slightly and the top is golden.

Remove from the oven and set the cheese and toast rounds onto the tossed salad.

MAKES 12

SPRING ROLLS

A perennial Chinese favorite has moved front and center to the cocktail hour! Make them smaller as hors d'oeuvres, or full size as a starter. Either way, ensure that there is plenty of plum or sweet and sour sauce for dipping.

PREPARATION TIME: 50 minutes plus 4 hours resting time for the dough
COOKING TIME: 20 minutes

WRAPPERS
1 cup bread flour
1 egg, beaten
Cold water

FILLING
8oz pork, trimmed and finely
    shredded

4oz shrimp, shelled and chopped
4 green onions, finely chopped
2 tsps chopped fresh ginger
4oz Chinese cabbage leaves,
    shredded
3½oz bean sprouts
1 tbsp light soy sauce
Dash sesame seed oil
1 egg, beaten

To prepare the wrappers, sift the flour into a bowl and make a well in the center. Add the beaten egg and about 1 tbsp cold water. Begin beating with a wooden spoon, gradually drawing in the flour from the outside to make a smooth dough. Add more water if necessary.

Knead the dough until it is elastic and pliable. Place in a covered bowl and chill for about 4 hours or overnight.

When ready to roll out, allow the dough to come back to room temperature. Flour a large work surface well and roll the dough out to about ¼ inch thick.

Cut the dough into 12 equal squares and then roll each piece into a larger square about 6x6 inches. The dough should be very thin. Cover while preparing the filling.

Cook the pork in a little of the frying oil for about 2-3 minutes. Add the remaining filling ingredients, except the beaten egg, cook for a further 2-3 minutes and allow to cool.

Lay out the wrappers on a clean work surface with the point of each wrapper facing you. Brush the edges lightly with the beaten egg.

Divide the filling among all 12 wrappers, placing it just above the front point. Fold over the sides like an envelope.

Then fold over the point until the filling is completely covered. Roll up as for a jelly roll. Press all the edges to seal well.

Heat the oil in a deep fat fryer or in a deep pan to 375°F. Depending upon the size of the fryer, place in 2-4 spring rolls and fry until golden brown on both sides. The rolls will float to the surface when one side has browned and should be turned over. Drain thoroughly on paper towels and serve hot.

SERVES 8-10

A GREEN-PEAS SOUP

This is a summery version of a hearty winter staple. Green peas and mint add a freshness and a light, delicate taste to dried split peas.

PREPARATION TIME: 30 minutes

COOKING TIME: 45-50 minutes

¾ cup dried split peas
1¼lbs frozen peas
1½ cups fresh mint leaves

½ cup butter or margarine, melted
Pinch salt and pepper
Sprigs of fresh mint to garnish

Place the split peas with about 6 cups water in a heavy saucepan. Cover, bring to the boil and cook until very tender, about 40 minutes.

Strain the peas and reserve the liquid.

Pour the liquid back into the saucepan and add the frozen peas. Chop the mint leaves, reserving some for garnish, and add to the peas. Bring to the boil in a covered saucepan.

Meanwhile, add the melted butter to the dried peas and push through a strainer or work in a food processor to form a smooth purée. Add the purée to the green peas, mixing well. Add salt and pepper to taste.

Pour the hot soup into a tureen and garnish with sprigs or leaves of mint. Serve immediately.

SERVES 4

MELON AND PROSCIUTTO

The marriage of ripe melon with the richness of this Italian ham has become one of our best loved starters, no matter what season.

PREPARATION TIME: 20 minutes

1 large ripe melon	16 thin slices prosciutto ham

Cut the melon in half lengthways, scoop out the seeds and discard them.
    Cut the melon into quarters and carefully pare off the rind. Cut each quarter into four slices.
    Wrap each slice of melon in a slice of prosciutto and place on a serving dish. Alternatively, place the melon slices on the dish and cover with the slices of prosciutto, leaving the ends of the melon showing. Serve immediately.

SERVES 6-8

SUNNY GAZPACHO

A soup of Spanish heritage, this is the perfect summer first course. Use the sunripened surplus from your garden or market to achieve a truly authentic taste.

PREPARATION TIME: 20 minutes plus 2 hours for the soup to chill in the refrigerator

---

1 medium green pepper, seeded and roughly chopped
8 medium tomatoes, peeled, seeded and roughly chopped
1 large cucumber, peeled and roughly chopped
1 large onion, roughly chopped
3-5oz French bread, crusts removed
3 tbsps red wine vinegar
3 cups water
Pinch salt and pepper

1-2 cloves garlic, crushed
3 tbsps olive oil
2 tsps tomato paste (optional)

GARNISH
1 small onion, diced
½ small cucumber diced, but not peeled
3 tomatoes, peeled, seeded and diced
½ green pepper, seeded and diced

Combine all the prepared vegetables in a deep bowl and add the bread, breaking it into small pieces by hand. Mix together thoroughly.

Add the vinegar, water, salt, pepper and garlic.

Pour the mixture, a third at a time, into a blender or food processor and purée for about 1 minute, or until the soup is smooth.

Pour the purée into a clean bowl and gradually beat in the olive oil using a whisk. Add enough tomato paste for a good red color.

Cover the bowl tightly and refrigerate for at least 2 hours, or until thoroughly chilled. Before serving, whisk the soup to make sure all the ingredients are blended and then pour into a large chilled soup tureen or into chilled individual soup bowls. Serve all the garnishes in separate bowls to be added to the soup if desired.

At Kings Landing Historical Settlement, carefully restored clapboard buildings are a part of the recreation of a 19th-century New Brunswick community.

SERVES 4-6

FETTUCINE ESCARGOTS WITH LEEKS AND SUN-DRIED TOMATOES

The rich, concentrated flavor of sun-dried tomatoes adds a pungent touch to pasta dishes in particular. Try making your own using perfectly red, ripe tomatoes or buy them packed in oil for a taste of the sun all year long. Here, the combination with escargots and leeks is sheer inspiration!

PREPARATION TIME: 24 hours for the tomatoes to dry

COOKING TIME: 15-20 minutes

---

6 sun-dried tomatoes or 6 fresh Italian plum tomatoes
14oz canned escargots (snails), drained
12oz fresh or dried whole-wheat fettucine (tagliatelle)
3 tbsps olive oil
2 cloves garlic, crushed
1 large or 2 small leeks, trimmed, split, well washed and finely sliced

6 oyster, shittake or other large mushrooms
4 tbsps chicken or vegetable stock
3 tbsps dry white wine
6 tbsps heavy cream
2 tsps chopped fresh basil
2 tsps chopped fresh parsley
Salt and pepper

To "sun-dry" tomatoes in the oven, cut the tomatoes in half lengthwise.

Use a teaspoon or your finger to scoop out about half the seeds and juice. Press gently with your palm to flatten slightly. Sprinkle both sides with salt and place tomatoes, cut side up, on a rack over a baking pan.

Place in the oven on the lowest possible setting, with door ajar, if necessary, for 24 hours, checking after 12 hours. Allow to dry until no liquid is left and the tomatoes are firm. Chop roughly.

Drain the escargots well and dry with paper towels.

Place the fettucine in boiling salted water and cook for about 10-12 minutes, or until al dente. Drain, rinse under hot water and leave in a colander to drain dry.

Meanwhile, heat the olive oil in a frying pan and add the garlic and leeks. Cook slowly to soften slightly. Add the mushrooms and cook until the leeks are tender crisp. Remove to a plate. Add the drained escargots to the pan and cook over high heat for about 2 minutes, stirring constantly.

Pour on the stock and wine and bring to the boil. Boil to reduce by about a quarter and add the cream and tomatoes. Bring to the boil then cook slowly for about 3 minutes. Add the herbs, salt and pepper to taste. Add the leeks, mushrooms and fettucine to the pan and heat through. Serve immediately.

Nahanni National Park in the Northwest Territories has some spectacular scenery, and although difficult to reach, it is very popular with adventure enthusiasts.

SERVES 8-10

MINESTRONE

Generations of Canadians have grown up coming home to steaming bowls of this favorite Italian soup. Our version substitutes potatoes for pasta and is hearty enough to serve as a nourishing meal.

PREPARATION TIME: 20 minutes plus overnight soaking for the beans

COOKING TIME: 2 hours

8 oz dried white cannellini beans
2 tbsps olive oil
1 large ham bone, preferably
   prosciutto
1 onion, chopped
2 cloves garlic, crushed
4 sticks celery, sliced
2 carrots, diced
1 small head Savoy cabbage or
   1lb fresh spinach, well washed
4oz green beans, cut into 1 inch
   lengths
8oz tomatoes, peeled, seeded and
   diced

1 dried red chili pepper
10 cups water (or half beef stock)
1 sprig fresh rosemary
1 bay leaf
3 potatoes, peeled and cut into small
   dice
3 zucchini, trimmed and cut into
   small dice
1 tbsp chopped fresh basil
1 tbsp chopped fresh parsley
Grated Parmesan cheese
Salt and pepper

Place the beans in a large bowl, cover with cold water and leave to soak overnight.

Heat the oil in a large stock pot and add ham bone, onion and garlic. Cook until onion has softened but not colored. Add the celery, carrots, cabbage and green beans. If using spinach, reserve until later.

Drain the beans and add them to the pot with the tomatoes and the chili pepper. Add the water and bring to the boil, skimming the surface as necessary. Add the rosemary and bay leaf and simmer, uncovered, until the beans are tender, about 1¼ hours.

Add the potatoes and cook for the further 20 minutes.

Add the zucchini and spinach and cook, skimming the surface, about 20 minutes longer. Remove the ham bone, rosemary and bay leaf and add basil and parsley. Season and serve with Parmesan cheese.

Facing page: the unspoilt tranquility of Kingsmere Lake, in Prince Albert National Park, clearly illustrates the importance of preserving Canada's areas of natural beauty.

SERVES 2-4

DEVILLED SEA SHRIMP

Although this delightful recipe hails from the coastal regions, it is popular everywhere these succulent shrimp are available.

PREPARATION TIME: 30 minutes

COOKING TIME: 15 minutes

2 dozen raw large shrimp, unpeeled	4oz cooked crab meat
4 tbsps butter or margarine	6 tbsps fresh breadcrumbs
1 small red pepper, seeded and finely chopped	1 tbsp chopped parsley
2 green onions, finely chopped	2 tbsps mayonnaise
½ tsp dry mustard	Salt and pepper
2 tsps dry sherry	1 small egg, beaten
1 tsp Worcestershire sauce	Grated Parmesan cheese
	Paprika

Remove all of the shrimp shells except for the very tail ends.

Remove the black veins on the rounded sides.

Cut the shrimp down the length of the curved side and press each one open.

Melt half the butter or margarine in a small pan and cook the pepper to soften, about 3 minutes. Add the green onions and cook a further 2 minutes.

Combine the peppers with the mustard, sherry, Worcestershire sauce, crab meat, breadcrumbs, parsley and mayonnaise. Add seasoning and enough egg to bind together.

Spoon the stuffing onto the shrimp and sprinkle with the Parmesan cheese and paprika. Melt the remaining butter or margarine and drizzle over the shrimp.

Bake in a pre-heated 350°F oven for about 10 minutes. Serve immediately.

SERVES 10
PÂTÉ DE CAMPAGNE QUÉBECOIS

Also known as pâté maison or country pâté, this French terrine embodies all of the rich and satisfying flavors so relished in old Quebec cookery. Make ahead to have on hand to serve during the holiday season!

PREPARATION TIME: 25 minutes plus refrigerating until firm

COOKING TIME: 2 hours

One of the largest French-speaking cities outside Paris, Montreal is a truly cosmopolitan city. It is *the* place to eat out, and a leading center of culture and style.

¾lb pork liver, skinned and ducts removed
¾lb, pork coarsely ground
4oz veal, coarsely ground
8oz pork fat, coarsely ground
1 clove garlic, crushed
2 shallots, finely chopped
8oz bacon strips, rind and bones removed

3 tbsps cognac
½ tsp ground allspice
Salt and freshly ground black pepper
1 tsp chopped fresh thyme or sage
4oz smoked tongue or ham, cut into ¼ inch cubes
2 tbsps heavy cream
1 large bay leaf

Preheat the oven to 350°F.

Place the liver in a food processor and process once or twice to chop roughly. Add the ground meats and fat, shallots, garlic, cognac, allspice, salt and pepper and thyme and process once or twice to mix. Do not over-work the mixture; it should be coarse.

Stretch the strips of bacon with the back of a knife and line a terrine, metal baking pan or ovenproof glass dish. Stir the cream and the cubed tongue or ham into the meat mixture by hand and press it into the dish on top of the bacon.

Place the bay leaf on top and fold over any overlapping edges of bacon.

Cover the dish with a tight-fitting lid or two layers of foil and place the dish in a bain marie (dish of hand hot water) to come halfway up the sides of the terrine. Bake the pâté for 2 hours or until the juices are clear. When it is done, remove it from the oven and remove the foil or lid.

Cover with fresh foil and weight down the pâté with cans of food or balance scale weights. Allow to cool at room temperature and then refrigerate the pâté, still weighted, until completely chilled and firm.

To serve, remove the weights and foil. Turn the pâté out and scrape off the fat. Slice through the bacon into thin slices.

SERVES 6-8

CLAM CHOWDER

French fishermen are credited with the origins of this rich soup-stew, but the settling Acadians adopted it as their own, using the many delicious varieties of clams found along the Eastern seaboard.

PREPARATION TIME: 30 minutes

COOKING TIME: 20 minutes

2lbs clams (1lb shelled or canned clams)	6 medium potatoes, peeled and cubed
3oz rindless bacon, diced	Salt and pepper
2 medium onions, finely diced	4 cups milk
1 tbsp flour	1 cup light cream
	Chopped parsley (optional)

Scrub the clams well and place them in a basin of cold water with a handful of flour to soak for 30 minutes. Drain the clams and place them in a deep saucepan with about ½ cup cold water. Cover and bring to the boil, stirring occasionally until all the shells open. Discard any shells that do not open. Strain the clam liquid and reserve it and set the clams aside to cool.

Place the diced bacon in a large, deep saucepan and cook slowly until the fat is rendered. Turn up the heat and brown the bacon. Remove it to paper towels to drain.

Add the onion to the bacon fat in the pan and cook slowly to soften. Stir in the flour and add the potatoes, salt, pepper, milk and reserved clam juice.

Cover and bring to the boil and cook for about 10 minutes, or until the potatoes are nearly tender. Remove the clams from their shells and chop them if large. Add to the soup along with the cream and diced bacon. Cook a further 10 minutes, or until the potatoes and clams are tender. Add the chopped parsley, if desired, and serve immediately.

Fishing is an integral part of life for many people in the delightful coastal villages of Nova Scotia.

The crafts and lifestyle of a bygone age are practised at Kings Landing Historical Settlement.

SERVES 6-8

CREAM OF PUMPKIN SOUP

Pumpkins have a special place in Canadian culinary history. This soup, with its excellent color and texture, makes a distinctive first course, especially if you serve it in its shell.

PREPARATION TIME: 45 minutes

COOKING TIME: 20 minutes

1 large pumpkin about 4-5lbs in weight
¼ cup butter or margarine
1 large onion, sliced

1 cup heavy cream
Pinch salt, white pepper and nutmeg
Snipped chives to garnish

Wash the pumpkin well on the outside and cut through horizontally, about 2 inches down from the stem end.

Carefully cut most of the pulp off the top and reserve the "lid" for later use.

Remove the seeds from the inside and discard them.

Using a small, sharp knife, carefully remove all but ½ inch of the pulp from inside the pumpkin. Work slowly and carefully to avoid piercing the outer skin of the pumpkin. Chop all the pulp from the top of the pumpkin and the inside and set it aside.

Melt the butter or margarine in a large saucepan and add the onion. Cook slowly until the onion is tender but not brown. Add the pumpkin flesh and about 4 cups cold water. Bring to the boil and then allow to simmer gently, covered, for about 20 minutes.

Purée the mixture in a food processor or blender in several small batches. Return the soup to the pot and add the cream, salt, pepper and nutmeg to taste. Reheat the soup and pour it into the reserved pumpkin shell. Garnish the top of the soup with snipped chives, if desired, before serving.

SERVES 6

SAVORY PARTY TARTS

Packaged pastry makes these tasty tarts very easy. They make excellent appetizers, snacks or even a light meal with a salad. Try substituting smoked salmon and dill for an elegant alternative.

PREPARATION TIME: 30 minutes

COOKING TIME: 25 minutes

8oz package phyllo pastry
¾ cup butter, melted
8oz sprue (thin asparagus)
4oz feta cheese
½ cup plain yogurt

2 eggs, beaten
3 green onions, finely chopped
1 tbsp chopped mint
Salt and pepper

Use a tart tin with 12 spaces or use 12 ramekin dishes. Cut the pastry in squares large enough to fill the pans or dishes, with enough to overlap the tops by about 1 inch.

Layer 3 sheets of pastry, each brushed with melted butter. Cut into 3 inch squares and stack 3 squares, turning each slightly to make a frilled edge. Carefully push the pastry into buttered tart tins or ramekins and keep covered while preparing the filling.

Cut the sprue into 1 inch pieces, leaving the tips whole. Cook in boiling salted water until just tender. Rinse under cold water and allow to drain completely. Mix together thoroughly the cheese, yogurt, eggs, onions, mint, salt and pepper. Stir in the drained sprue and fill the pastry to within ½ inch of the top.

Bake in a preheated 375°F oven for about 25 minutes or until the pastry is crisp and golden and the filling is set and risen. Allow to cool for about 10 minutes and them remove to a serving dish.

Deer are a common sight in Elk Island National Park; a home they share with over thirty other species of mammals, including bison, beaver and, of course, elk.

SERVES 4

CHICKEN LIVER SALAD

Delicately flavored with shallots and parsley, this salad is quick, economical and absolutely delicious.

PREPARATION TIME: 40 minutes

COOKING TIME: 5 minutes

---

12 chicken livers
1 shallot or 2 green onions, finely
    chopped
3 tbsps Xeres or wine vinegar
2 cloves garlic, finely chopped
1 tbsp parsley

4 slices white bread
1 tomato, cut into small dice
¼ cup butter
⅓ cup olive oil
4 small servings of shredded mixed
    green salad

Cut the slices of bread into small, even-sized cubes.

Heat 2 tbsps olive oil in a frying pan and quickly fry the bread cubes over a high heat. Fry until lightly golden and then tip out onto paper towels to drain.

Melt the butter in the same pan and gently fry the chicken livers.

Once the livers are cooked through (cut one to check that the centers are not too pink), add the shallot, garlic and parsley.

Fry for a few minutes and then deglaze the pan with 2 tbsps vinegar.

Place the prepared green salad onto 4 plates and tip the livers evenly over the 4 plates.

Mix together the remaining vinegar, olive oil and a little salt and pepper. Shake or stir well to form a vinaigrette dressing.

Sprinkle the diced tomato and the croutons over the chicken livers and pour over a little dressing. The dish can be served immediately, or you may prefer to serve when the livers are cold.

SERVES 6-8

LENTIL SOUP WITH SAUSAGE

Take the edge off a frosty fall day with this richly flavored soup of German origins. Vary the sausage to suit your own taste.

PREPARATION TIME: Lentils need 3-4 hours to soak

COOKING TIME: 1½ hours total cooking time

12oz brown or Egyptian lentils, well washed
4oz Canadian back bacon, derinded and chopped
1 onion, thinly sliced
4 sticks celery, sliced
2 carrots, peeled and thinly sliced

3 tbsps butter or margarine
3-4 bratwurst, cut into 1 inch pieces
1 tbsp flour
2 tsps wine vinegar
Salt and pepper
1 cup water or stock

Soak the lentils in a large bowl or stock pot with enough water to cover, for 3-4 hours. Drain and place in a large stock pot. Add the bacon, onion, celery and 3½ cups water. Bring to the boil, cover and simmer for 45 minutes.

When lentils are almost cooked, melt the butter in a frying pan and fry the bratwurst until brown. Remove and set aside. Stir the flour into the butter in the pan and gradually whisk in the additional water or stock. Bring to the boil, stirring continuously. Add the vinegar and seasonings and allow to boil for about 1 minute.

Stir the mixture into the soup, blending thoroughly. Bring back to the boil and then allow the soup to simmer, uncovered, for a further 40-50 minutes, or until the lentils are completely tender. Add the bratwurst and heat through.

SERVES 6-8

CRAB MEAT BALLS

Delicious as a first course or a cocktail snack, crab meat balls can be made ahead, then coated and fried at the last minute.

PREPARATION TIME: 40-50 minutes

COOKING TIME: 3 minutes per batch of 6

1lb fresh or frozen crab meat, chopped finely

4 slices white bread, crusts removed and made into crumbs

1 tbsp butter or margarine

1 tbsp flour

½ cup milk

½ red or green chili, seeded and finely chopped

1 green onion, finely chopped

1 tbsp chopped parsley

Salt

Flour

2 eggs, beaten

Dry breadcrumbs

Oil for frying

Combine the crab meat with the fresh breadcrumbs and set aside.

Melt the butter and add the flour off the heat. Stir in the milk and return to moderate heat. Bring to the boil, stirring constantly.

Stir the white sauce into the crab meat and breadcrumbs, adding the chili, onion, and parsley. Season with salt to taste, cover and allow to cool completely.

Shape the cold mixture into 1 inch balls with floured hands.

Coat with beaten egg using a fork to turn balls in the mixture or use a pastry brush to coat with egg.

Coat with the dry breadcrumbs.

Fry in oil in a deep sauté pan, saucepan or deep-fat fryer at 350°F until golden brown and crisp, about 3 minutes per batch of 6. Turn occasionally while frying.

Drain on paper towels and sprinkle lightly with salt.

Unusual rock formations and beautifully clear waters attract many visitors to Flowerpot Island, one of the prettiest of the Georgian Bay Islands.

SERVES 4-6

FRENCH ONION SOUP AU GRATIN

Originally a Parisian speciality, this savory recipe for onion soup has evolved into a classic of our own French-Canadian cuisine. The secret of its deep, rich flavor is in the long, slow cooking of the onions.
Bon appetit!

PREPARATION TIME: 20 minutes

COOKING TIME: 50-60 minutes in total

¼ cup butter or margarine
2lbs onions, peeled and thinly sliced
2 tsps sugar
Pinch salt and pepper
1½ tbsps flour
1 tsp dried thyme
7 cups brown stock
½ cup dry white wine

CRÔUTES
12 1 inch slices French bread
1 tbsp olive oil
2 cups grated Gruyère cheese

Melt the butter in a large saucepan over a moderate heat. Stir in the onions and add the sugar. Cook, uncovered, over low heat, stirring occasionally, for 20-30 minutes or until the onions are golden brown.

Sprinkle the flour over the onions and cook for 2-3 minutes. Pour on the stock and stir to blend the flour. Add salt, pepper and thyme and return the soup to low heat. Simmer, partially covered, for another 30-40 minutes. Allow the soup to stand while preparing the crôutes.

Brush each side of the slices of bread lightly with olive oil and place them on a baking sheet. Bake in a preheated oven, 325°F, for about 15 minutes. Turn the slices over and bake for a further 15 minutes, or until the bread is dry and lightly browned.

To serve, skim fat from the soup and ladle soup into a tureen or individual soup bowls. Place the crôutes on top of the soup and sprinkle over the grated cheese. Place the soup in a hot oven and bake for 10-20 minutes, or until the cheese has melted. Brown under a preheated broiler, if desired, before serving.

A Canadian National Railways train carefully makes its way across the North Thompson River in British Columbia.

SERVES 4

IMPERIAL ASPARAGUS

One of the first signs of spring and a sure sign that you care for your guests. Be sure to pare the stalks, as this makes their delicate flavor even more exquisite. Add a royal touch with just a drizzle of this beautifully enriched white wine sauce!

PREPARATION TIME: 30 minutes

COOKING TIME: 22-25 minutes

2lbs white asparagus
3 tbsps butter or margarine
3 tbsps flour
1 cup chicken stock or asparagus
   cooking liquid

½ cup German style white wine
2 egg yolks
4 tbsps heavy cream
Salt and pepper
Pinch sugar

The dome of St. Joseph's Oratory has been a Montreal landmark since its completion in the 1930s.

Trim the ends of the asparagus to remove the top parts and to make the spears the same length. Using a swivel vegetable peeler, pare the stalks up to the tips.

To cook the asparagus, tie the spears in a bundle and stand them upright in a deep saucepan of lightly salted boiling water. Alternatively, place the spears in a large sauté pan of boiling salted water. If using a sauté pan, place half on and half off the heat, with the tips of the asparagus off the heat.

Cook, uncovered, for about 12-15 minutes, or until the asparagus is tender. Drain and reserve the cooking liquid. Keep the asparagus warm in a covered serving dish.

To prepare the sauce, melt the butter in a heavy-based saucepan and stir in the flour off the heat. Gradually beat in the asparagus cooking liquid or chicken stock and add the wine. Stir until the sauce is smooth and then place over a low heat.

Bring the sauce to the boil, stirring constantly, and allow to boil for about 1-2 minutes, or until thickened.

Beat the egg yolks and cream together and add a few spoonfuls of the hot sauce. Return the egg and cream mixture to the pan, stirring constantly. Reheat if necessary, but do not allow the sauce to boil once the egg is added. Add salt and white pepper and a pinch of sugar if desired. Pour over the asparagus to serve.

CHAPTER
2
Light Meals and Snacks

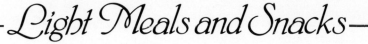

Previous pages: the curving crest of Ontario's Horseshoe Falls, over whose ledge the Niagara's thundering waters drop over 160 feet.

SERVES 4

SUNSHINE EGGS

A lighter variation on the 'eggs for brunch' theme that is tasty, satisfying and a delight to behold.

PREPARATION TIME: 45 minutes

COOKING TIME: 10-15 minutes

1½lbs fresh spinach	**HOLLANDAISE SAUCE**
1½ tbsps butter or margarine	3 egg yolks
1 tbsp flour	⅔ cup unsalted butter
1 cup milk	1 tbsp lemon juice
Salt, pepper and nutmeg	Pinch salt and pepper
4 artichoke hearts, quartered	1 large piece canned pimento,
4 eggs	drained and cut into thin strips

Strip the spinach leaves from the stalks and wash the leaves well. Place the leaves in a large saucepan and add a pinch of salt. Cover the pan and cook the spinach over moderate heat in only the water that clings to the leaves. When the spinach is just wilted, take off the heat and drain well. Chop roughly and set aside.

Melt the butter or margarine in a medium-sized saucepan and stir in the flour. Gradually add the milk, whisking constantly, and place the sauce over low heat. Whisk the sauce as it comes to the boil and allow it to boil rapidly for about one minute to thicken. Stir in the spinach and season the sauce with salt, pepper and nutmeg. Add the artichoke hearts and set the sauce aside.

Fill a large sauté pan with water and bring to the boil. Turn down the heat and, when the water is just barely simmering, break an egg into a cup or onto a saucer. Gently lower the egg into the water to poach. Repeat with the remaining eggs. Poach over gentle heat, never allowing the water to boil. Alternatively, cook in a special poaching pan. Cook until the whites have set but the yolks are still soft. Remove the eggs from the pan with a draining spoon and place in cold water until ready to use.

Place the egg yolks in a food processor or blender with the lemon juice and seasoning. Process once or twice to mix. Place the butter in a small saucepan and melt over gentle heat. Turn up the heat and when the butter is bubbling, take off the heat. With the machine running, gradually pour the butter onto the eggs in a very thin but steady stream.

To assemble the dish, reheat the spinach sauce and place an equal amount of it on each plate. Make a well in the center. Place the eggs back into hot water briefly to reheat, and drain well. Place an egg in the hollow of the spinach sauce on each plate. Spoon over some of the Hollandaise sauce to coat each egg completely. Make a cross with two strips of pimento on top of each egg and serve immediately.

The magnificent bald eagle graces many of the national parks and wilderness areas of Canada.

SERVES 4

GREEN GODDESS SALAD

The cool green herby dressing mingles yet never masks the delicate flavors of avocado, chicken or seafood in this updated version of a luncheon classic.

PREPARATION TIME: 30 minutes

8 anchovy fillets, soaked in milk, rinsed and dried
1 green onion, chopped
2 tbsps chopped fresh tarragon
3 tbsps chopped chives
4 tbsps chopped parsley
1 cup prepared mayonnaise
½ cup natural yogurt

2 tbsps tarragon vinegar
Pinch sugar and cayenne pepper
1 large head lettuce
1lb cooked chicken or seafood
1 avocado, peeled and sliced or cubed
1 tbsp lemon juice

Combine all the ingredients, except the lettuce, avocado and chicken or shellfish in a food processor. Work the ingredients until smooth, well mixed and green. Leave in the refrigerator at least 1 hour for the flavors to blend.

Shred the lettuce or tear into bite-size pieces and arrange on plates.

Top the lettuce with the cooked chicken cut into strips or cubes. If using crab or lobster, cut the meat into bite-size pieces. Shelled shrimp or mussels can be left whole.

Spoon the dressing over the chicken or seafood. Brush the avocado slices or toss the cubes with lemon juice and garnish the salad. Serve any remaining dressing separately.

MAKES 1 OMELET

FRESH TOMATO OMELET

Never out of fashion, the omelet makes an easy summer fresh appetizer or lunch. This one is especially pretty with its ripe tomatoes and fresh herbs.

PREPARATION TIME: 25 minutes

COOKING TIME: 2-3 minutes

1lb tomatoes
½ tsp chopped fresh oregano or
   basil

Salt and pepper
4 eggs, lightly beaten
3 tbsps oil

To make the tomatoes easier to peel, drop them into boiling water and leave them for about 5 seconds. Remove them with a draining spoon and put immediately into ice cold water. Peel with a sharp knife.

Cut the tomatoes in half and remove the seeds and juice with a teaspoon. Cut the tomato halves into thin strips.

Beat the eggs with the herbs, salt and pepper and heat the oil in a large frying pan. When the oil is hot, pour in the eggs and stir with a spatula for about 2-3 minutes, or until the eggs are cooked but not completely set. Sprinkle over the tomato strips and cook until just heated through. Sprinkle with chopped parsley, if desired, before serving.

Outside Calgary's Education Center stands the intriguing *Family of Man* sculpture by Mario Armengol.

This wonderfully evocative Indian mask can be found in Victoria's Heritage Court Complex, alongside many other ancient woodcarvings by Pacific Coast Indians.

SERVES 6-12

SPINACH AND FETA PIE

Serve this classic Greek cheese pie anytime a light, savory nibble is required. Packaged pastry makes it simplicity itself.

PREPARATION TIME: 25 minutes

COOKING TIME: 40 minutes

1lb package phyllo pastry
1 cup butter, melted
2lbs fresh spinach
2 tbsps olive oil
2 onions, finely chopped

3 tbsps chopped fresh dill
Salt and pepper
3 eggs, slightly beaten
2 cups feta cheese, crumbled

Preheat the oven to 375°F. Unfold the pastry on a flat surface and cut it to fit the size of the baking dish to be used. Keep the pastry covered.

Tear the stalks off the spinach and wash the leaves well. Shred the leaves with a sharp knife.

Heat the oil in a large sauté pan and cook the onions until soft. Add the spinach and stir over a medium heat for about 5 minutes. Turn up the heat to evaporate any moisture.

Allow the spinach and onions to cool. Mix in the dill, eggs, salt, pepper, and cheese.

Melt the butter and brush the baking dish on the bottom and sides. Brush top sheet of phyllo pastry and place it in the dish. Brush another sheet and place that on top of the first. Repeat to make 8 layers of pastry.

Spread on the filling and cover the top with 6 or 7 layers of pastry, brushing each layer with melted butter. Brush the top layer well and score the pastry in square or diamond shapes. Do not cut through to the bottom layer.

Sprinkle with water and bake for 40 minutes or until crisp and golden.

Leave the pie to stand for about 10 minutes and then cut through the scoring completely to the bottom layer. Lift out the pieces to a serving dish.

Spanning the St. Lawrence River is the Ogdensberg International Bridge, which crosses to the United States at Johnstown.

SERVES 6-8

SEAFOOD TORTA

A very stylish variation of a fish flan or pie, this dish makes a lovely light supper with an aperitif and a salad. Simply vary the seafood to suit the occasion and your budget.

PREPARATION TIME: 40 minutes plus 1 hours refrigeration for pastry

COOKING TIME: 40 minutes

PASTRY
2 cups all-purpose flour, sifted
½ cup unsalted butter
Pinch salt
4 tbsps cold milk

FILLING
4oz whitefish fillets (plaice, sole or cod)
8oz cooked shrimp
4oz flaked crab meat

½ cup white wine
½ cup water
Large pinch hot pepper flakes
Salt and pepper
2 tbsps butter
2 tbsps flour
1 clove garlic, crushed
2 egg yolks
½ cup heavy cream
Chopped fresh parsley

To prepare the pastry, sift the flour into a bowl or onto a work surface. Cut the butter into small pieces and begin mixing them into the flour. Mix until the mixture resembles fine breadcrumbs – this may also be done in a food processor. Make a well in the flour, pour in the milk and add the pinch of salt. Mix with a fork, gradually incorporating the butter and flour mixture from the sides until all the ingredients are mixed. This may also be done in a food processor.

Form the dough into a ball and knead for about 1 minute. Leave the dough in the refrigerator for about 1 hour.

To prepare the filling, cook the whitefish fillets in the water and wine with the red pepper flakes for about 10 minutes or until just firm to the touch. When the fish is cooked, remove it from the liquid and flake it into a bowl with the shrimp and the crab meat. Reserve the cooking liquid.

Melt the butter in a small saucepan and stir in the flour. Gradually strain on the cooking liquid from the fish, stirring constantly until smooth. Add garlic, place over high heat and bring to the boil. Lower the heat and allow to cook for 1 minute. Add to the fish in the bowl and set aside to cool.

On a well-floured surface, roll out the pastry and transfer it with a rolling pin to a tart pan with a removable base. Press the dough into the pan and cut off any excess. Prick the pastry base lightly with a fork and place a sheet of wax paper inside. Fill with rice, dried beans or baking beans and chill for 30 minutes. Bake the pastry shell blind for 15 minutes in a 375°F oven.

While the pastry is baking, combine the egg yolks, cream and parsley and stir into the fish filling. Adjust the seasoning with salt and pepper. When the pastry is ready, remove the paper and beans and pour in the filling.

Return the tart to the oven and bake for a further 25 minutes. Allow to cool slightly and then remove from the pan. Transfer to a serving dish and slice before serving.

TANGY TACOS

North of the border, Mexican food is enjoying tremendous popularity, as restaurants proliferate and prepared ingredients appear on the supermarket shelves, spreading the hot news! Everybody likes the easy, make your own informality of the Mexican buffet; not least of all because of the fresh and spicy new flavor combinations that result. Try one and see!

12 taco shells

BEEF FILLING
1 tbsp oil
1lb ground beef
1 medium onion, chopped
2 tsps ground cumin
1 clove garlic, crushed
2 tsps chili powder
Pinch paprika
Salt and pepper

CHICKEN FILLING
3 tbsps butter or margarine
1 medium onion, chopped
1 small red pepper, seeded and
    chopped
2 tbsps sliced almonds

12oz chicken breasts, skinned and
    finely chopped
Salt and pepper
1 piece fresh ginger, peeled and
    chopped
6 tbsps milk
2 tsps cornstarch
½ cup sour cream

TOPPINGS
Shredded lettuce
Grated cheese
Tomatoes, seeded and chopped
Chopped green onions
Avocado slices
Sour cream
Jalapeno peppers
Taco sauce

Heat oil for beef filling in a large frying pan and brown the beef and onions, breaking the meat up with a fork as it cooks. Add spices, garlic and seasoning and cook about 20 minutes. Set aside.

Melt the 2 tbsps butter or margarine in a medium saucepan and add the onion. Cook slowly until softened.

Add the red pepper and almonds and cook slowly until the almonds are lightly browned. Stir often during cooking. Remove to a plate and set aside.

Melt the remaining butter in the same saucepan and cook the chicken for about 5 minutes, turning frequently. Season and return the onion mixture to the pan along with the chopped ginger.

Blend the milk and cornstarch and stir into the chicken mixture. Bring to the boil and stir until very thick. Mix in the sour cream and cook gently to heat through. Do not boil.

Heat the taco shells on a baking sheet in a preheated 350°F oven for 2-3 minutes. Place on the sheet with the open ends down.

To fill, hold the shell in one hand and spoon in about 1 tbsp of either beef or chicken filling.

Next, add a layer of shredded lettuce, followed by a layer of grated cheese.

Add choice of other toppings and finally spoon on some taco sauce.

MAKES ½ PINT

TACO SAUCE

This basic recipe has many uses in Mexican cooking – sauce, topping, dip or as an ingredient to give a dish extra flavor.

PREPARATION TIME: 15-20 minutes

COOKING TIME: 8-10 minutes

1 tbsp oil	½ tsp ground coriander
1 onion, sliced	½ clove garlic, crushed
1 green pepper, diced	Pinch salt, pepper and sugar
½-1 red or green chili pepper	14oz canned tomatoes
½ tsp ground cumin	Tomato paste (optional)

This patchwork of multi-colored fields is part of a large Mennonite Village Museum at Steinbach, Manitoba, where the early farming methods and lifestyle of Mennonite settlers has been faithfully reconstructed.

Heat the oil in a heavy-based saucepan and when hot, add the onion and pepper. Cook slowly to soften slightly.

Chop the chili and add with the cumin, coriander, garlic and cook a further 2-3 minutes.

Add sugar, seasonings and tomatoes with their juice. Break up the tomatoes with a fork or a potato masher.

Cook a further 5-6 minutes over moderate heat to reduce and thicken slightly. Add tomato paste for color, if necessary. Adjust seasoning and use hot or cold according to your recipe.

SERVES 6-8

MAPLE BAKED BEANS

An old time winter warm-up dish that still pleases young and old alike. Serve straight from the pot with lots of buttered steamed brown bread to accompany. For a hearty, more traditional meal serve simply with sausages on the side.

PREPARATION TIME: 20 minutes plus overnight soaking for the beans

COOKING TIME: 3½ hours

1lb dried navy or white pea beans	1 tsp dry mustard
5 cups water	¾-1 cup maple syrup
4oz salt pork or slab bacon	Salt and pepper
1 onion, peeled and left whole	

Soak the beans overnight in the water. Transfer to fresh water to cover. Bring to the boil and allow to cook for about 10 minutes. Drain and reserve the liquid.

Place the beans, salt pork or bacon and whole onion in a large, deep casserole or bean pot. Mix the syrup, mustard, salt and pepper with 1 cup of the reserved bean liquid. Stir into the beans and add enough bean liquid to cover. Expose only the pork rind on the salt pork and cover the casserole.

Bake in a pre-heated 300°F oven for about 2 hours. Add the remaining liquid, stirring well, and cook a further 1½ hours, or until the beans are tender. Uncover the beans for the last 30 minutes.

To serve, remove and discard the onion. Take out the salt pork or bacon and remove the rind. Slice or dice the meat and return to the beans. Check the seasoning and serve.

Additional maple syrup may be passed in a pitcher.

Right: the flower of the prickly pear cactus, pictured in Grasslands National Park, Saskatchewan.

MAKES 1 LOAF

STEAMED BROWN BREAD

The classic accompaniment to Maple Baked Beans. It's traditional to bake it in a can! Serve warm with butter or cream cheese.

PREPARATION TIME: 20 minutes

COOKING TIME: 3-4 hours

1½ cups fine cornmeal
2 cups whole-wheat flour
1 cup all-purpose flour
Pinch salt
⅓ cup molasses mixed with 1 tsp
  bicarbonate of soda

1½ cups cold water
Butter or oil
Boiling water

Sift the dry ingredients into a large bowl and return the bran to the bowl.

Mix the molasses, bicarbonate of soda and water together. Make a well in the center of the flour and pour in the mixture. Mix just until well blended.

Use a large can from canned tomatoes, coffee or canned fruit. Alternatively, use about 6 smaller cans. Wash them well and remove the labels. Grease generously with oil or butter. Spoon the bread mixture to come about two thirds of the way up the sides of the cans.

Cover the tops of the cans tightly with buttered or oiled foil. Place them on a rack in a deep saucepan. Pour enough boiling water around the cans to come about halfway up the sides. Allow water to bubble gently to steam the bread for 3-4 hours in the covered pan. Add more boiling water as necessary during cooking.

The bread is ready when a skewer inserted into the center of the bread comes out clean.

SERVES 8-10

NACHOS

Spicy is hot! These nachos make super cocktail savories that never fail to excite taste buds and temperaments! Experiment with your own toppings.

PREPARATION TIME: 25 minutes

1 package round tortilla chips	**TACO FILLING**
1 can refried beans	2 tsps oil
1 can Jalapeno bean dip	8oz ground beef
Full quantity Taco Sauce recipe	2 tsps chili powder
8-10 cherry tomatoes, sliced	Pinch ground coriander
½ cup sour cream or natural yogurt	Pinch cayenne pepper
Sliced black and stuffed green olives	Salt and pepper
Grated Cheddar cheese	

Prepare taco filling as for Tacos recipe. Top half of the tortilla chips with refried beans and half with beef taco filling.

Place a spoonful of taco sauce on the bean-topped chips and Jalapeno bean dip in the beef-topped chips.

Top the tortilla chips with tomatoes, sour cream or yogurt, olives or cheese in any desired combination, and serve.

SERVES 4

PENNE WITH HAM AND ASPARAGUS

Penne refers to the Italian pasta shaped like pens or quills. Served in smaller amounts as a starter, or more generously with a green salad, this dish is so simple yet sophisticated it truly is worth writing home about!

PREPARATION TIME: 20 minutes

COOKING TIME: 20 minutes in total

8oz penne
12oz fresh asparagus
4oz cooked ham

2 tbsps butter or margarine
1 cup heavy cream

Using a swivel vegetable peeler, scrape the sides of the asparagus spears starting about 2 inches from the top. Cut off the ends of the spears about 1 inch from the bottom.

Cut the ham into strips about ½ inch thick.

Bring a sauté pan of water to the boil, adding a pinch of salt. Move the pan so it is half on and half off direct heat. Place in the asparagus spears so that the tips are off the heat. Cover the pan and bring back to the boil. Cook the asparagus spears for about 2 minutes. Drain and allow to cool.

Cut the asparagus into 1 inch lengths, leaving the tips whole.

Melt the butter in the sauté pan and add the asparagus and ham. Cook briefly to evaporate the liquid, and add the cream. Bring to the boil and cook for about 5 minutes to thicken the cream.

Meanwhile, cook the pasta in boiling salted water with 1 tbsp oil for about 10-12 minutes.

Drain the pasta and rinse under hot water. Toss in a colander to drain and mix with the sauce. Serve with grated Parmesan cheese, if desired.

SERVES 4

PIZZA WITH PEPPERS, OLIVES & ANCHOVIES

For a time known mainly as a "fast food" snack, pizza has resumed it rightful place as a stylish, versatile and ever popular food to suit all tastes and mealtimes. Our recipe has a specific topping but you may like to try your own favorites, the only limit is your imagination!

PREPARATION TIME: 40 minutes

COOKING TIME: 30 minutes

PIZZA DOUGH
½oz fresh yeast
½ tsp sugar
¾ cup lukewarm water
2 cups all-purpose flour
Pinch salt
2 tbsps oil

TOPPING
2 tsps olive oil
1 onion, finely chopped
1 clove garlic, crushed

1lb canned tomatoes
1 tbsp tomato paste
½ tsp each oregano and basil
1 tsp sugar
Salt and pepper
½ red pepper
½ green pepper
½ cup black olives, pitted
2oz canned anchovies, drained
1 cup Mozzarella cheese, grated
2 tbsps grated Parmesan cheese

Cream the yeast with the sugar in a small bowl, add the lukewarm water and leave to stand for 10 minutes to prove. Bubbles will appear on the surface when ready.

Sift the flour and salt into a bowl, make a well in the center and add the oil and the yeast mixture. Using a wooden spoon, beat the liquid in the center of the well, gradually incorporating the flour from the outside until it forms a firm dough.

Turn the dough out onto a floured surface and knead for 10 minutes, or until the dough is smooth and elastic. Place in a lightly oiled bowl or in a large plastic bag, cover or tie the bag and leave to stand in a warm place for 30 minutes, or until the dough has doubled in bulk.

Knock the dough back and knead it into a smooth ball. Flatten the dough and roll out into a circle on a floured surface. The circle should be about 10 inches in diameter.

To prepare the topping, heat the oil in a heavy-based saucepan and add the onion and the garlic. Cook until the onion and garlic have softened but not colored. Add the tomatoes and their juice, tomato paste, herbs, sugar, salt and pepper. Bring the sauce to the boil and then allow to simmer, uncovered, to reduce. Stir the sauce occasionally to prevent sticking. When the sauce is thick and smooth, leave it to cool. Spread the cooled sauce over the pizza dough. Sprinkle half the cheese on top of the tomato sauce and then arrange the topping ingredients. Sprinkle with remaining cheese and bake in a 400°F oven for 15-20 minutes or until the cheese is melted and bubbling and the crust if brown.

Low tide exposes seaweed and rocks on a quiet beach at Broad Cove, Nova Scotia.

SERVES 8

GUACAMOLE

The rich delicate flavor of avocados combines with cool tomatoes, lime and herbs to create one of the most famous Mexican accompaniments known. Serve on its own as a starter, or with other Mexican recipes.

PREPARATION TIME: 25 minutes

1 medium onion, finely chopped	1 tbsp chopped fresh coriander
1 clove garlic, crushed	Pinch salt
Grated rind and juice of ½ lime	Coriander leaves to garnish
½ quantity Taco Sauce recipe	1 package tortilla chips
3 large avocados	

Mix the onion, garlic, rind and juice of lime and the taco sauce together in a large mixing bowl.

Cut the avocados in half lengthwise. Twist the halves gently in opposite directions to separate.

Hit the stone with a large, sharp knife and twist the knife to remove the stone.

Place the avocado halves cut side down on a chopping board. Lightly score the skin lengthwise and gently pull back to peel. Alternatively, scoop out avocado flesh with a spoon, scraping the skin well.

Chop the avocado roughly and immediately place in the bowl with the onion and lime.

Use a potato masher to break up the avocado until almost smooth. Do not over-mash. Season with salt and stir in the chopped coriander. Spoon into a serving bowl and garnish with coriander leaves.

Surround the bowl with tortilla chips for dipping.

MAKES 5 CUPS

LEMONADE

Team up a cold glass of fresh lemonade with the spicy tastes of Mexico, serve at barbeques or carry in a flask for a tangy refresher at picnics. Nothing beats it!

PREPARATION TIME: 20 minutes

---

1 lemon	Maraschino cherries
¾ cup sugar	Lemon slices
4½ cups water	

Wash the lemon well and cut into small pieces, removing the seeds. Place in a blender or food processor with the sugar and 1 cup water.

Blend until smooth, add remaining water and mix well.

Pour into ice-filled glasses or into a pitcher filled with ice and garnish with the cherries and lemon slices.

SERVES 6

APPLE FILLED PANCAKES

Apples have always had pride of place in Canadian cookery, and these light, fluffy pancakes of German origin combine the two cultures deliciously. Be sure to use a cooking apple such as Cortland or Northern Spy for best results, then serve for brunch or as a treat with coffee.

PREPARATION TIME: 30 minutes

COOKING TIME: 5-6 minutes per pancake
10 minutes for the filling

FILLING	PANCAKES
3 tbsps butter or margarine	4 eggs
1½ lbs cooking apples, peeled, cored and cut into ¼-inch-thick wedges	1½ cups milk
	½ cup all-purpose flour
2 tbsps brown sugar	½ tbsp sugar
½ tsp ground allspice	Pinch salt
	6 tbsps butter or margarine
	Powdered sugar

Melt the butter for the filling in a large frying pan over moderate heat. When just foaming, add the apples and sprinkle with sugar and allspice. Cook, stirring occasionally, until the apples are lightly browned and slightly softened. Put the apples aside while preparing the batter.

Combine the eggs and the milk in a large bowl and whisk thoroughly. Sift the flour with the sugar and salt and add to the eggs gradually, whisking constantly. Alternatively, combine all the ingredients in a food processor and work until just smooth.

To cook the pancakes, melt 1 tbsp of butter over moderate heat in an 8 inch frying pan. Pour in about ½ cup of the batter and swirl the pan from side to side so that the batter covers the base.

Scatter over some of the filling and cook the pancake for about 3 minutes.

Pour another ½ cup of the batter over the apples and place under a preheated broiler for about 1-2 minutes, or until the top is golden brown and firm to the touch.

Loosen the sides and the base of the pancake and slide it onto a heated serving dish. Add 1 tbsp of butter to the pan for each pancake. Just before serving, sprinkle the pancakes with the powdered sugar.

Overleaf: Riel House, a beautifully restored home built by the family of Manitoba's founding father, Louis Riel.

CHAPTER
3
Main Course Meats

SERVES 4

VEAL SCALOPPINE WITH PROSCIUTTO AND CHEESE

No longer confined to your favorite trattoria, this deceptively simple entrée can be recreated by using the fresh ingredients now widely available in neighborhood speciality shops. Good veal is tender and quick cooking, but expensive, so save this recipe for your next dinner party!

PREPARATION TIME: 15 minutes

COOKING TIME: 15-20 minutes

8 veal escalopes	8 slices Mozzarella cheese
2 tbsps butter or margarine	3 tbsps sherry
1 clove garlic, crushed	½ cup beef stock
1 sprig rosemary	Salt and pepper
8 slices prosciutto ham	

Pound the veal escalopes out thinly between two pieces of wax paper with a meat mallet or a rolling pin.

Melt the butter or margarine in a sauté pan and add the veal and garlic. Cook until the veal is lightly browned on both sides.

Place a piece of prosciutto on top of each piece of veal and add the sherry, stock and sprig of rosemary to the pan. Cover the pan and cook the veal for about 10 minutes over gentle heat, or until done.

Remove the meat to a heatproof serving dish and top each piece of veal with a slice of cheese.

Bring the cooking liquid from the veal to the boil and allow to boil rapidly to reduce slightly.

Meanwhile, broil the veal to melt and brown the cheese. Remove the sprig of rosemary from the sauce and pour the sauce around the meat to serve.

People all over the world see the Mounties as representative of Canada's early pioneer days. Today, the Royal Canadian Mounted Police still plays an important role in the policing of most of Canada's provinces.

SERVES 6

NAVARIN PRINTANIER

Celebrate spring's arrival with this rich and flavorful casserole made with tender lamb chops and surrounded by the season's first fresh vegetables.

PREPARATION TIME: 30-40 minutes

COOKING TIME: 30-35 minutes

⅓ cup vegetable oil
12 even-sized lamb cutlets
Flour mixed with salt, pepper and a pinch dried thyme
2 shallots or leeks, finely chopped
1 clove garlic, crushed
2 cups brown stock
½ cup dry white wine
5 tomatoes, peeled, seeded and coarsely chopped
1 bouquet garni

SPRING VEGETABLES

12 new potatoes, scrubbed but not peeled
8 baby carrots, scraped (if green tops are in good condition, leave on)
6 small turnips, peeled and left whole
12oz frozen petits pois
8oz green beans cut into 1 inch lengths on the diagonal
12 green onions, roots ends trimmed and green tops trimmed about 3 inches from the ends
1 tbsp chopped parsley (optional)

Preheat the oven to 350°F. Heat about half the oil in a large, heavy-based frying pan. Dredge the lamb cutlets with the flour mixture, shaking off the excess. Brown the lamb cutlets 4 at a time, adding more oil if necessary. When the cutlets are brown on all sides, remove them to a heavy casserole.

Remove most of the oil from the pan and cook the shallots and garlic over moderate heat, stirring constantly. Add the stock and bring to the boil, scraping the bottom of the pan to remove the browned meat juices. Allow to boil rapidly to reduce slightly, then add the tomatoes.

Pour the sauce over the lamb, turning the cutlets to coat all of them with the sauce. Add the bouquet garni, cover tightly and cook in the oven for about 30 minutes, or until the lamb is tender.

After about 10 minutes, add the potatoes and carrots to the lamb.

Add the turnips, green beans, peas and green onions 15 minutes before the end of cooking time.

After 30 minutes, remove the lamb and any vegetables that are tender. Boil the sauce rapidly to reduce it and cook any vegetables that need extra time. Pour the sauce over the lamb and vegetables to serve and sprinkle with chopped parsley, if desired.

Brightly colored fields of rape are a wonderful sight alongside the farm buildings at Fairview, Alberta .

SERVES 2-3

BEEF WITH BROCCOLI

The arrival of the Canadian Pacific Railway in Western Canada brought the first Chinese immigrants to Canada and along with them a whole new world of cooking arts found its way into our Canadian cuisine. Over time, the oriental methods for stir-frying and many of the recipes have been integrated as well. In this recipe, stir-frying the sliced beef ensures a tender, tasty main course. Delicious served with fried rice.

PREPARATION TIME: 25 minutes

COOKING TIME: 4 minutes

1lb rump steak, partially frozen	8oz fresh broccoli
4 tbsps dark soy sauce	6 tbsps oil
1 tbsp cornstarch	1 inch piece ginger, peeled and
1 tbsp dry sherry	shredded
1 tsp sugar	Salt and pepper

Trim any fat from the meat and cut into very thin strips across the grain. Strips should be about 3 inches long.

Combine the meat with the soy sauce, cornstarch, sherry and sugar. Stir well and leave long enough for the meat to completely defrost.

Trim the flowerets from the stalks of the broccoli and cut them into even-sized pieces. Peel the stalks of the broccoli and cut into thin, diagonal slices.

Slice the ginger into shreds. Heat a wok and add 2 tbsps of the oil to it. Add the broccoli and sprinkle with salt. Stir-fry, turning constantly, until the broccoli is dark green. Do not cook for longer than 2 minutes. Remove from the wok and set aside.

Place the remaining oil in the wok and add the ginger and beef. Stir-fry, turning constantly, for about 2 minutes. Return the broccoli to the pan and mix well. Heat through for 30 seconds and serve immediately.

Sun-bleached moose antlers adorn the walls of a weatherboarded building near Dawson, in the Yukon.

Left: Beef with
Broccoli.
Overleaf:
spectacular
mountain views are
a common feature in
Yoho National Park.

MAKES 6-8

FRIED RICE

*A basic recipe for a traditional Chinese accompaniment to
stir-fried dishes, this can be more substantial with the addition
of meat, poultry or seafood.*

COOKING TIME: 10 minutes for the rice to cook,
20 minutes for it to drain as dry as possible
4 minutes for the fried rice dish

1lb cooked rice, well drained and dried	2oz cooked peas
3 tbsps oil	2 green onions, thinly sliced
1 egg, beaten	Dash sesame oil
1 tbsp soy sauce	Salt and pepper

Heat a wok and add the oil. Pour in the egg and soy sauce and cook until just
beginning to set.
    Add the rice and peas and stir to coat with the egg mixture. Allow to cook
for about 3 minutes, stirring continuously. Add seasoning and sesame oil.
    Spoon into a serving dish and sprinkle over the green onions.

Facing page: gently rounded hills and dense forests are a distinct feature of Quebec's La Mauricie National Park, here viewed from Le Passage lookout.

SERVES 4-6

PORK FILLET WITH PRUNES

A refined dish of French heritage which is worthy of your most important guests.

PREPARATION TIME: 25 minutes

COOKING TIME: 45 minutes

2-3 small pork tenderloins	1-2 tbsps flour
1lb pitted prunes	Salt and pepper
2 cups white wine	1 tbsp redcurrant jelly
3 tbsps butter or margarine	1 cup heavy cream

Soak the prunes in the white wine for about 1 hour and then put them into a very low oven to soften further. If the prunes are the ready-softened variety, soak for 20 minutes and omit the oven cooking.

Slice the pork fillet on the diagonal into 1-inch-thick pieces. Flatten them slightly with the palm of the hand. Dredge them with the flour and melt the butter in a heavy pan. When the butter is foaming, put in the pork and cook until lightly browned on both sides. It may be necessary to cook the pork fillet in several batches.

Add half the soaking liquid from the prunes, cover the pan and cook very gently on moderate heat for about 45 minutes. If necessary, add more wine from the prunes while the pork is cooking.

When the pork is tender, pour liquid into a small saucepan and bring to the boil. Reduce by about ¼ and add the redcurrant jelly. Stir until dissolved and then add the cream. Bring the sauce back to the boil and allow to boil rapidly, stirring frequently. When the sauce is reduced and thickened slightly, pour over the meat and reheat. Add the prunes and transfer to a serving dish. Sprinkle with chopped parsley if desired.

SERVES 8-10

MAPLE GLAZED HAM

This rich tasting and deeply colored ham has provided the centerpiece for generations of traditional family meals and get-togethers from coast to coast. Its appeal never fails.

PREPARATION TIME: 30 minutes

COOKING TIME: 1½-2 hours

7-11lb precooked Virginia ham
1 tbsp ground cloves
1 tbsp cinnamon
½ cup brown sugar

1 cup maple syrup
1 cup water
Whole cloves

Preheat oven to 350°F.

Remove skin from ham and score fat in diamond pattern. Rub with the cinnamon and cloves, then cover evenly with the brown sugar. If desired, decorate with whole cloves. Place in the roasting pan, then pour the combined maple syrup and water around the ham.

Bake the ham for approximately 90 minutes, basting every 20 minutes using a large spoon or a baster. (Add water as necessary to prevent the syrup from caramelizing.) Cover loosely with foil if the ham begins to brown too much.

A ready to eat ham is done when its internal temperature registers 138°F/59°C. Allow to stand 15 minutes before serving.

Newfoundland, Canada's easternmost province, has an exciting variety of scenery, from towering waterfalls to beautiful, silent forests.

Left: Maple Glazed Ham.

SERVES 6

SWEET POTATO PUDDING

This sweet potato pudding is a traditional accompaniment to maple glazed ham, but try serving it with poultry as well. It could also be served as a sweet pudding, topped with whipped or ice cream.

PREPARATION TIME: 25 minutes

COOKING TIME: 45 minutes-1 hour

2 medium-size sweet potatoes	1 tsp cinnamon
2 cups milk	¼ cup pecans, roughly chopped
2 eggs	2 tbsps butter
¾ cup sugar	6 tbsps dark rum

Peel the potatoes and grate them coarsely. Combine with the milk.

Beat the eggs and gradually add the sugar, continuing until light and fluffy. Combine with the cinnamon and the pecans.

Stir into the potatoes and milk and pour the mixture into a lightly buttered shallow baking dish. Dot with the remaining butter.

Bake about 45 minutes to 1 hour in a pre-heated 350°F oven. Bake until the pudding is set and then pour over the rum just before serving.

SERVES 4-6

LIVER VENEZIANA

Canadians of Italian descent have enjoyed this famous dish from the northern region of Italy for generations. It has many variations, but do try the original for a superbly satisfying meal. A creamy risotto is the ideal accompaniment.

PREPARATION TIME: 10 minutes

COOKING TIME: 30 minutes

RISOTTO
9oz Italian rice
3 tbsps butter or margarine
1 large onion, chopped
4 tbsps dry white wine
2 cups chicken stock
¼ tsp saffron
2 tbsps grated fresh Parmesan
   cheese
Salt and pepper

LIVER
1lb calves' or lambs' liver
Flour for dredging
3 onions, thinly sliced
2 tbsps butter or margarine
3 tbsps oil
Salt and pepper
Juice of ½ a lemon
1 tbsp chopped parsley

Melt the butter for the risotto in a large sauté pan, add the onion and cook until soft but not colored, over gentle heat.

Add the rice and cook for a minute until the rice looks clear.

Add the wine, stock, saffron and seasoning. Stir well and bring to the boil. Lower the heat and cook gently, stirring frequently until the liquid has evaporated. This will take about 20 minutes.

Meanwhile, skin the liver and cut out any large tubes.

Cut the liver into strips and toss in a sieve with the flour to coat.

Heat the butter or margarine and 1 tbsp oil in a large sauté or frying pan. Cook the onions until golden. Remove the onions from the pan to a plate. Add more oil if necessary, raise the heat under the pan and add the liver. Cook, stirring constantly, for about 2 minutes. Return the onions and add the lemon juice and parsley. Cook a further 2 minutes or until the liver is done. Season with salt and pepper and serve with the risotto.

To finish the risotto, add the cheese and salt and pepper to taste when the liquid has evaporated, and toss to melt the cheese.

SERVES 4

LAMB STEAKS WITH EGGPLANT AND PEPPERS

Eggplant or aubergine, once a staple used only in mid-Eastern and Mediterranean cuisines, is now happily at home in North America. In this dish, rich with the aromas of garlic and herbs, eggplant partners perfectly with tender lamb steaks.

PREPARATION TIME: 1 hour

COOKING TIME: 20 minutes

4 large or 8 small round bone lamb steaks
4 tbsps olive oil
1 clove garlic, crushed
1 sprig fresh rosemary

1 small red pepper, seeded and cut into 1 inch pieces
2 shallots, chopped
4 tbsps olive oil
2 tsps chopped parsley

Black pepper
1 tbsp red wine vinegar
1 large eggplant
Salt
1 small green pepper, seeded and
    cut into 1 inch pieces

2 tsps chopped fresh marjoram
6 tbsps dry white wine
Salt and pepper

Place lamb in a shallow dish with the oil, garlic, rosemary, pepper and vinegar and turn frequently to marinate for 1 hour.

Cut the eggplant in half and score lightly. Sprinkle with salt and leave to stand on paper towels for about 30 minutes. Rinse well and pat dry.

Cut eggplant in 1 inch pieces. Heat more oil in a frying pan and add the eggplant. Cook, stirring frequently, over moderate heat until lightly browned. Add peppers, shallots and herbs, and cook a further 5 minutes.

Add the wine and bring to the boil. Cook quickly to reduce the wine. Set the mixture aside.

Meanwhile, place the lamb on a broiler pan, reserving the marinade. Cook under a pre-heated broiler for 10 minutes per side. Baste frequently with the marinade. Lamb may be served pink inside.

Serve the lamb with the eggplant accompaniment.

Left: the fresh beauty of First Vermilion Lake in Banff National Park, Alberta.
Overleaf: a peaceful scene at Blue Rocks, near Lunenburg, Nova Scotia.

CHAPTER
4
Fish and Seafood

15853

SERVES 4

EAST COAST BOUILLABAISE

French settlers brought this favorite recipe to the New World and just as they would have at home, they used local, seasonal ingredients in it. The method remains the same today!

PREPARATION TIME: 35 minutes

COOKING TIME: 30 minutes

STOCK
1lb fish bones, skin and heads
7 cups water
1 small onion, thinly sliced
1 small carrot, thinly sliced
1 bay leaf
6 black peppercorns
1 blade mace
1 sprig thyme
2 lemon slices

BOUILLABAISE
⅓ cup butter or margarine
1 carrot, sliced

3 leeks, well washed and thinly
   sliced
1 clove garlic
Pinch saffron
⅓-½ cup dry white wine
8oz canned tomatoes
1 lobster
1lb cod or halibut fillets
1lb mussels, well scrubbed
1lb small clams, well scrubbed
8 new potatoes, scrubbed but not
   peeled
Chopped parsley
8oz large shrimp, peeled and
   deveined

First prepare the fish stock. Place all the ingredients in a large stock pot and bring to the boil over high heat. Lower the heat and allow to simmer for 20 minutes. Strain and reserve the stock. Discard the fish bones and vegetables.

Melt the butter in a medium-sized saucepan and add the carrots, leeks and garlic. Cook for about 5 minutes until slightly softened.

Add the saffron and wine and allow to simmer for about 5 minutes.

Add the fish stock along with all the remaining bouillabaise ingredients except the shrimp. Bring the mixture to the boil and cook until the lobster turns red, the mussel and clam shells open and the potatoes are tender. Turn off the heat and add the shrimp. Cover the pan and let the shrimp cook in the residual heat. Divide the ingredients among 4 soup bowls. Remove the lobster and cut it in half. Divide the tail between the other 2 bowls and serve the bouillabaise with garlic bread.

SERVES 4

GRILLED TROUT WITH PEPPER RELISH

Fresh trout, perfectly grilled, and spicy sweet pepper relish make an unusual, innovative and very special dish.

PREPARATION TIME: 10 minutes

COOKING TIME: 10 minutes

---

1 lime
2 tbsps butter, melted
4 filleted trout, unskinned (double fillets preferred)

8 tbsps prepared hot pepper relish
Lime wedges or coriander leaves to garnish

Remove the rind of the lime with a citrus zester and set it aside.

Squeeze the juice and mix with the butter.

Place the fish fillets on a grill rack and baste with the butter and lime juice mixture. Place under a pre-heated grill for about 4-5 minutes, depending on the thickness of the fillets. Baste frequently.

Pour over any remaining butter and lime juice and sprinkle the fish with the lime zest.

Gently re-heat the relish and spoon 2 tbsps down the center of each of the double fillets. Garnish with lime or coriander.

Left: a magnificent sunset over Banff National Park, where the rugged wilderness of the Rockies meets with lowland valleys and lush alpine meadows.

SERVES 4

WHOLE BAKED SALMON WITH MARITIME STUFFING

A whole fish, perfectly cooked and stuffed with oysters from an old fashioned maritime recipe will make a grand impression at the most stylish of functions. Try it for your next buffet or dinner party.

PREPARATION TIME: 25 minutes

COOKING TIME: 40 minutes

4¼lb whole fish, gutted and boned
(use Atlantic or Pacific salmon, or bass)

STUFFING
8oz savory cracker crumbs
¼ cup butter, melted

Pinch salt and pepper
2 tsps lemon juice
¼ tsp each dried thyme, sage and marjoram
1 shallot, finely chopped
10 oysters, shelled

Have the fishmonger gut and bone the fish, leaving on the head and tail. Rinse the salmon inside and pat dry.

Place the fish on lightly oiled foil. Combine all the stuffing ingredients, mixing so that the oysters do not fall apart.

Open the cavity of the fish and spoon in the stuffing.

Close the fish and pat out gently so that the stuffing is evenly distributed. Close the foil loosely around the fish and place it directly on the oven shelf or in a large roasting pan. Cook at 400°F for about 40 minutes. Unwrap the fish and slide it onto a serving plate. Peel off the top layer of skin if desired and garnish with lemon slices.

Cormorants sit on the red sandstone rocks at Orby Point, on Prince Edward Island.
Overleaf: fields of rape disappear over the horizon in the farmlands of Manitoba.

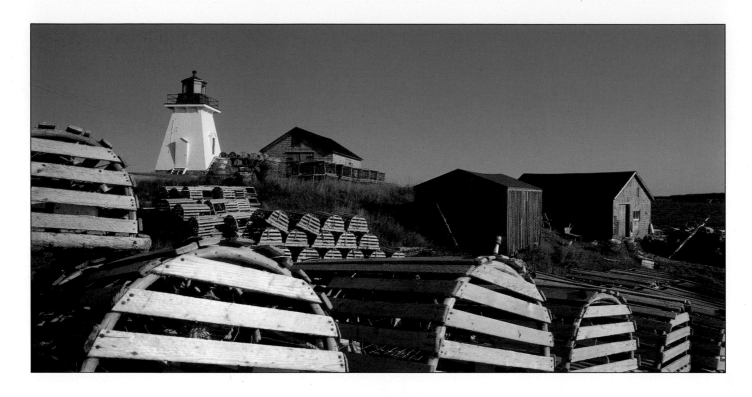

Fishermen's huts and lobster pots surround the lighthouse at Neil's Harbor, Cape Breton, Nova Scotia.

MAKES 4

BOILED NOVA SCOTIA LOBSTER

Any mariner worth his (or her) salt will agree that boiled lobster "in the rough" is the simplest and finest way to enjoy its sweet, succulent meat. Tie on your bib and mop up with plenty of fresh, crusty bread and melted butter.

COOKING TIME: 15 minutes

4 1lb lobsters	1 cup melted butter
Water	Lemon wedges
Salt or seaweed	Parsley sprigs

Fill a large stock pot full of water and add salt or a piece of seaweed. Bring the water to the boil and then turn off the heat.

Place the live lobsters into the pot, keeping your hand well away from the claws. Lower them in claws first.

Bring the water slowly back to the boil and cook the lobsters for about 15 minutes, or until they turn bright red.

Remove them from the water and drain briefly on paper towels. Place on plate and garnish the plate with lemon wedges and parsley sprigs. Serve with individual dishes of melted butter for dipping.

SERVES 4-6

FISHERMAN'S STEW

In the early days every coastal village had a variation of this quick, economical and satisfying fish stew. Then, the ingredients changed according to season and availability, but today not even a landlubber need do without!

PREPARATION TIME: 20 minutes

COOKING TIME: 45 minutes

6 tbsps olive oil	Pinch dried thyme
2 large onions, sliced	1½ cups water
1 red pepper, seeded and sliced	2lb whitefish fillets, skinned
4oz mushrooms, sliced	½ cup white wine
1lb canned tomatoes	2 tbsps chopped parsley
Pinch salt and pepper	

Heat the oil in a large saucepan and add the onions. Cook until beginning to look translusent. Add the pepper and cook until the vegetables are softened.

Add the mushrooms and the tomatoes and bring the mixture to the boil.

Add thyme, salt, pepper and water and simmer for about 30 minutes.

Add the fish and wine and cook until the fish flakes easily, about 15 minutes. Stir in parsley.

To serve, place a piece of toasted French bread in the bottom of the soup bowl and spoon over the fish stew.

Right: the crescent-shaped towers of Toronto's City Hall, designed by Finnish architect Viljo Revell and internationally acclaimed since their completion in 1965.

SERVES 4

SWORDFISH FLORENTINE

Swordfish, with it dense texture, is a perfect and healthful substitute for meat. Here is a distinctly Mediterranean flavor.

PREPARATION TIME: 25 minutes

COOKING TIME: 6-8 minutes

4 swordfish steaks about 6-8oz each in weight
Salt, pepper and lemon juice
Olive oil
2lbs fresh spinach, stems removed and leaves well washed

AIOLI SAUCE
2 egg yolks
1-2 cloves garlic
Salt, pepper and dry mustard
Pinch cayenne pepper
1 cup olive oil
Lemon juice or white wine vinegar

Sprinkle fish with pepper, lemon juice and olive oil. Place under a preheated broiler and cook for about 3-4 minutes per side. Fish may also be cooked on an outdoor barbeque grill.

Meanwhile, use a sharp knife to shred the spinach finely. Place in a large saucepan and add a pinch of salt. Cover and cook over moderate heat with only the water that clings to the leaves after washing. Cook about 2 minutes, or until leaves are just slightly wilted. Set aside.

Place egg yolks in a food processor, blender or cup of a hand blender. Add the garlic, crushed, if using a hand blender. Process several times to mix eggs and purée garlic. Add salt, pepper, mustard and cayenne pepper. With the machine running, pour oil through the funnel in a thin, steady stream. Follow manufacturer's directions if using a hand blender.

When the sauce becomes very thick, add some lemon juice or vinegar in small quantities.

To serve, place a bed of spinach on a plate and top with the swordfish. Spoon some of the aioli sauce on top of the fish and serve the rest separately.

SERVES 4

WEST COAST SHRIMP AND SCALLOP STIR-FRY

Stir-frying is the perfect way to cook seafood. This dish typifies much of the fresh cooking that is coming from the west coast today, light, elegant and lovely to look at.

PREPARATION TIME: 35 minutes

COOKING TIME: 8-10 minutes

3 tbsps oil
4 tbsps pine nuts
1lb uncooked shrimp
1lb shelled scallops, quartered if large
2 tsps grated fresh ginger
1 small red or green chili, seeded and finely chopped
2 cloves garlic, finely chopped
1 large red pepper, seeded and cut into 1 inch diagonal pieces

8oz fresh spinach, stalks removed and leaves well washed and shredded
4 green onions, cut in ½ inch diagonal pieces
4 tbsps fish or chicken stock
4 tbsps light soy sauce
4 tbsps rice wine or dry sherry
1 tbsp cornstarch

Heat oil in a wok and add the pine nuts. Cook over low heat, stirring continuously until lightly browned. Remove with a draining spoon and drain on paper towels.

Add the shrimp and scallops to the oil remaining in the wok and stir over moderate heat until shellfish is beginning to look opaque and firm and the shrimp look pink.

Add the ginger, chili, garlic and red pepper and cook a few minutes over moderately high heat.

Add the spinach and onion, and stir-fry briefly. Mix the remaining ingredients together and pour over the ingredients in the wok.

Turn up the heat to bring the liquid quickly to the boil, stirring ingredients constantly. Once the liquid thickens and clears, stir in the pine nuts and serve immediately.

This picturesque church nestles among the trees in Mont-Tremblant, Quebec.

SERVES 4

TUNA BAKED IN PARCHMENT

Cooking "en papillote" is an old French technique now enjoying great vogue as a healthful cooking method which is particularly good with fish. Try this recipe with salmon or halibut steaks.

PREPARATION TIME: 35 minutes

COOKING TIME: 10-12 minutes

4 tuna steaks, about 8oz each in weight
1 red onion, thinly sliced
1 beefsteak tomato, cut in 4 slices
1 green pepper, seeded and cut in thin rings
8 large, uncooked peeled shrimp

2 tsps finely chopped fresh oregano
1 small green or red chili, seeded and finely chopped
4 tbsps dry white wine or lemon juice
Salt
Oil

Lightly oil 4 oval pieces of baking parchment about 8×10 inches.

Place a tuna steak on half of each piece of parchment and top with 2 slices of onion.

Place a slice of tomato on each fish and top with green pepper rings.

Place 2 shrimp on top and sprinkle over the oregano, salt and chili pepper.

Spoon the wine or lemon juice over each fish and fold the parchment over the fish.

Overlap the edges and pinch and fold to seal securely. Place the parcels on a baking sheet.

Bake for about 10-12 minutes in a pre-heated 400°F oven.

Unwrap each parcel at the table to serve.

The numerous lakes and forests of Prince Albert National Park, Saskatchewan, attract a multitude of outdoor enthusiasts.

SERVES 2

BARBECUED SHRIMP

It's the sauce rather than the cooking method that gives this dish its name. It's spicy, zippy and hot.

PREPARATION TIME: 15 minutes

COOKING TIME: 5 minutes

1lb large shrimp, cooked and
    unpeeled
½ cup unsalted butter
1 tsp each white, black and cayenne
    pepper
Pinch salt
1 tsp each chopped fresh thyme,
    rosemary and marjoram

1 clove garlic, crushed
1 tsp Worcestershire sauce
½ cup fish stock
4 tbsps dry white wine
Cooked rice or Green rice

Remove the eyes and the legs from the shrimp.

Melt the butter in a large frying pan and add the white pepper, black pepper, cayenne pepper, herbs and garlic. Add the shrimp and toss over heat for a few minutes. Remove the shrimp and set them aside.

Add the Worcestershire sauce, stock and wine to the ingredients in the pan. Bring to the boil and cook for about 3 minutes to reduce. Add salt to taste.

Arrange the shrimp on a bed of rice and pour over the sauce to serve.

SERVES 6

GREEN RICE

Fresh herbs are a must for this rice dish, but use whatever mixture suits your taste or complements the main course. A lovely color with the Barbecued Shrimp!

PREPARATION TIME: 20 minutes

COOKING TIME: 20-25 minutes

2 tbsps oil	3oz mixed chopped fresh herbs
2 tbsps butter	(parsley, thyme, marjoram, basil)
¾ cup uncooked long-grain rice	1 small bunch green onions, finely
2 cups boiling water	chopped
Pinch salt and pepper	

Heat the oil in a large, heavy-based saucepan and add the butter. When foaming, add the rice and cook over moderate heat for about 2 minutes, stirring constantly.

When the rice begins to look opaque, add the water, salt and pepper and bring to the boil, stirring occasionally.

Cover the pan and reduce the heat. Simmer very gently, without stirring, for about 20 minutes or until all the liquid has been absorbed and the rice is tender.

Chop the herbs very finely and stir into the rice along with the chopped green onions. Cover the pan and leave to stand for about 5 minutes before serving.

SERVES 4

CRISPY MARINATED FISH

The crispy crumb coating hides the extra flavor concealed in these special fish fillets. The lemon herb butter adds an extra tang over all.

PREPARATION TIME: 1 hour for fish to marinate

COOKING TIME: 6 minutes

8 sole or plaice fillets	6 tbsps butter
2 tbsps dry vermouth	1 clove garlic, crushed
1 bay leaf	2 tsps chopped parsley
6 tbsps olive oil	2 tbsps capers
Salt and pepper	1 tsp chopped fresh oregano
Seasoned flour for dredging	Juice of 1 lemon
2 eggs, lightly beaten	Salt and pepper
Dry breadcrumbs	Lemon wedges and parsley to
Oil for shallow frying	garnish

Skin the fillets with a sharp filleting knife. Remove any small bones and place the fillets in a large, shallow dish. Combine the vermouth, oil and bay leaf in a small saucepan and heat gently. Allow to cool completely and pour over the fish. Leave the fish to marinate for about 1 hour, turning them occasionally.

Remove the fish from the marinade and dredge lightly with the seasoned flour.

Dip the fillets into the beaten eggs to coat, or use a pastry brush to brush the eggs onto the fillets. Dip the egg-coated fillet into the breadcrumbs, pressing the crumbs on firmly.

Heat the oil in a large frying pan. Add the fillets and cook slowly on both sides until golden brown. Cook for about 3 minutes on each side, remove and drain on paper towels.

Pour the oil out of the frying pan and wipe it clean. Add the butter and the garlic and cook until both turn a light brown. Add the herbs, capers and lemon juice and pour immediately over the fish. Garnish with lemon wedges and sprigs of parsley.

SERVES 4

BLACKENED FISH

The popularity of this spice encrusted fish dish is on the rise; it comes from Cajun country, where every cook has their own special recipe for the spice mixture that 'blackens' the fillet. All agree, however, that to taste authentic, the crust should be very brown. Absolutely super with salmon!

PREPARATION TIME: 20 minutes

COOKING TIME: 4 minutes per fish

4 fish fillets, about 8oz each
1 cup unsalted butter
1 tbsp paprika
1 tsp garlic powder
1 tsp cayenne pepper

½ tsp ground white pepper
1 tsp finely ground black pepper
2 tsps salt
1 tsp dried thyme

Melt the butter and pour about half into each of four custard cups and set aside.

Brush each fish fillet liberally with the remaining butter on both sides.

Mix together the spices and thyme and sprinkle generously on each side of the fillets, patting it on by hand.

Heat a large frying pan and add about 1 tbsp butter per fish fillet. When the butter is hot, add the fish, skin side down first.

Turn the fish over when the underside is very brown and repeat with the remaining side. Add more butter as necessary during cooking.

When the top side of the fish is very dark brown, repeat with the remaining fish fillets, keeping them warm while cooking the rest.

Serve the fish immediately with the cups of butter for dipping.

Lion's Gate Bridge spans First Narrows, linking Vancouver with its residential suburbs to the north.
Overleaf: The sun seems almost reluctant to leave the dusky sky over Prince Edward Island.

CHAPTER
5
Poultry and Game

SERVES 4

CHICKEN WITH RED PEPPERS

Sweet roasted red pepper provides a vibrant accent of color and a spectacular tasting garnish when paired with chicken breasts in a dish that is easy to prepare, yet special enough for guests.

PREPARATION TIME: 35-40 minutes

COOKING TIME: 30 minutes

4 large red peppers	1 clove garlic, finely chopped
4 skinned and boned chicken breasts	3 tbsps white wine vinegar
1½ tbsps oil	2 green onions, finely chopped
Salt and pepper	Sage leaves for garnish

Cut the peppers in half and remove the stems, cores and seeds. Flatten the peppers with the palm of your hand and brush the skin sides lightly with oil.

Place the peppers skin side up on the rack of a pre-heated broiler and cook about 2 inches away from the heat source until the skins are well blistered and charred.

Wrap the peppers in a clean towel and allow them to stand until cool. Peel off the skins with a small vegetable knife. Cut into thin strips and set aside.

Place the chicken breasts between two sheets of plastic wrap and flatten by hitting with a rolling pin or meat mallet.

Heat 1½ tbsps oil in a large frying pan. Season the chicken breasts on both sides and place in the hot oil. Cook 5 minutes, turn over and cook until tender and lightly browned. Remove the chicken and keep it warm.

Add the pepper strips, garlic, vinegar and green onions to the pan and cook briefly until the vinegar loses its strong aroma.

Slice the chicken breasts across the grain into ¼ inch thick slices and arrange on serving plates. Spoon over the pan juices.

Arrange the pepper mixture with the chicken and garnish with the sage leaves.

Left: Vancouver's futuristic Expo Centre by night.

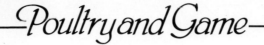

SERVES 4

COQ AU VIN

A wonderfully rich, cold weather meal that has travelled far from its original French Burgundian beginnings. For a pleasant change why not make it with one of the fine new Canadian red wines. Which ever wine you choose, make it a robust and hearty one, and serve it along with the dish for a truly memorable meal.

PREPARATION TIME: 30-40 minutes

COOKING TIME: 50 minutes

8oz thick cut bacon strips	1 bouquet garni
1½ cups water	1 clove garlic, crushed
2 tbsps butter or margarine	3 tbsps flour
12-16 button onions or shallots	1½ cups chicken stock
8oz mushrooms, left whole if small, quartered if large	2 tbsps chopped parsley
	4 slices bread, crusts removed
1½ cups dry red wine	Oil for frying
3lb chicken, cut into eight pieces	Salt and pepper
3 tbsps brandy	

Preheat oven to 350°F. Cut the bacon into strips about ¼ inch thick. Bring water to the boil and blanch the bacon by simmering for 5 minutes. Remove the bacon with a draining spoon and dry on paper towels. Re-boil the water and drop in the onions. Allow them to boil rapidly for 2-3 minutes and then plunge into cold water and peel. Set the onions aside with the bacon.

Melt half the butter in a large frying pan over moderate heat and add the bacon and onions. Fry over high heat, stirring frequently and shaking the pan, until the bacon and onions are golden brown. Remove them with a draining spoon and leave on paper towels. Add the remaining butter to the saucepan and cook the mushrooms for 1-2 minutes. Remove them and set them aside with the onions and bacon.

Right: Rue Petit Champlain, in Quebec City. The narrow streets and beautiful, historic buildings in the old town clearly show the French influence which is so much a part of Quebec's history.

Reheat the frying pan and brown the chicken, a few pieces at a time. When all the chicken is browned, transfer it to a large ovenproof casserole.

Pour the wine into a small saucepan and boil it to reduce to about 1 cup. Pour the brandy into a small saucepan or ladle and warm over low heat. Ignite with a match and pour the brandy (while still flaming) over the chicken. Shake the casserole carefully until the flames die down. If the brandy should flare up, cover quickly with the casserole lid. Add the bouquet garni and garlic to the casserole.

Pour off all but 1 tbsp of fat from the frying pan and stir in the flour. Cook over gentle heat, scraping any of the browned chicken juices from the bottom of the pan. Pour in the reduced wine and add the stock. Bring the sauce to the boil over high heat, stirring constantly until thickened. Strain over the chicken in the casserole and cover lightly.

Place in the oven and cook for 20 minutes. After that time, add the bacon, onions and mushrooms and continue cooking for a further 15-20 minutes, or until the chicken is tender. Remove the bouquet garni and season with salt and pepper.

Cut each of the bread slices into 4 triangles. Heat enough oil in a large frying pan to cover the triangles of bread. When the oil is very hot, add the bread triangles two at a time and fry until golden brown and crisp. Drain on paper towels. To serve, arrange the chicken in a deep dish, pour over the sauce and vegetables and arrange the fried bread croûtes around the outside of the dish. Sprinkle with chopped parsley.

SERVES 6-8

VENISON STEW

The Indians supplied venison to the settlers in return for salt pork, flour and sugar. The delicious result was rich and steaming roasts and stews, redolent of wood mushrooms and berries. Here, an updated recipe very similar to the old country stews of New France makes use of the abundant game found in the Canadian wilds.

PREPARATION TIME: 30 minutes plus overnight marinating

COOKING TIME: 2-2½ hours

3lbs venison shoulder or leg, cut into 2 inch pieces
2 cups dry red wine
4 tbsps red wine vinegar
1 bay leaf
2 tsps chopped fresh thyme or 1 tsp dried thyme
6 juniper berries, crushed
3 whole allspice berries
6 black peppercorns
1 clove garlic, crushed
4 tbsps oil
2 carrots, cut into strips
1 onion, thinly sliced
2 sticks celery, cut into strips
8oz mushrooms, sliced
Chopped parsley to garnish

Combine the wine, vinegar, bay leaf, thyme, juniper berries, allspice, peppercorns and garlic with the venison, and marinate overnight.

Remove the meat from the marinade and pat dry on paper towels. Reserve the marinade for later use.

Heat the oil in a heavy frying pan or casserole and brown the venison on all sides over very high heat. Brown in several small batches if necessary. Remove the venison and lower the heat. If using a frying pan, transfer the venison to an ovenproof casserole.

Lower the heat and brown the vegetables in the oil until golden. Sprinkle over the flour and cook until the flour browns lightly. Combine the vegetables with the venison and add the reserved marinade.

Cover and cook the stew in a pre-heated 300°F oven for about 2 hours.

Fifteen minutes before the end of cooking time, add the mushrooms and continue cooking until the meat is tender. Garnish with parsley before serving.

SERVES 4

APRICOT CHICKEN WITH MINT

This is a delicious recipe with a light yogurt-based sauce of the most beguiling pale apricot color and fascinating clear flavor. It can be served hot or cold.

PREPARATION TIME: 25 minutes plus at least 2 hours marinating

COOKING TIME: 45 minutes

8 chicken portions, skinned
2oz onion, finely chopped
1 orange
2 tbsps lemon juice
2oz dried apricots
2 tbsps chopped fresh mint or
   2 tsps dried mint

¼ pint dry white wine
Salt and freshly ground black pepper

TO SERVE
3-4 tbsps thick natural yogurt

Put the chicken into a flameproof casserole and add the onion, finely grated rind of the orange with 4 tablespoons of juice, and the remaining ingredients; be generous with the mint, as much of the flavor cooks away.

Cover and marinate for 2-4 hours at room temperature, or overnight in the refrigerator.

Preheat the oven to 375°F and bake the chicken, covered, for 45 minutes. Remove the chicken and keep warm.

Purée the rest of the casserole contents in a food processor or liquidiser and then force through a sieve (using the back of a soup ladle for efficiency and speed) into a saucepan.

Reheat but do not boil. Remove from the heat and stir in the yogurt, tasting all the time to get a pouring sauce that is rich but light in flavor – you will probably need 3-4 tablespoons of thick yogurt.

Adjust the seasoning with salt and pepper then pour the sauce over the chicken.

Irrigation has transformed the featureless prairies of Saskatchewan from arid grasslands to productive farmland.

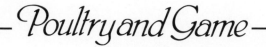

SERVES 2-3

DUCK IN CAPER SAUCE

A sweet and sour sauce with the tang of capers is a perfect accompaniment to a rich meat such as duck. Try this very tasty alternative to the usual fruit based garnishes.

PREPARATION TIME: 20 minutes plus 1-2 hours standing time for the duck

COOKING TIME: 1 hour

Below: a ferry on
Lake Ontario.

4½lb whole duck, giblets removed	4 tbsps sugar
1 clove garlic, crushed	½ cup water
Salt and pepper	1 tbsp vinegar or lemon juice
1 tbsp oil	6 tbsps capers
3 tbsps butter or margarine	4 tsps cornstarch mixed with 2 tbsps
1 cup chicken stock	water

Rub the cavity of the duck with the crushed garlic and sprinkle in salt and pepper. Leave to stand 1-2 hours but do not refrigerate.

Heat the oil in a heavy frying pan or roasting pan and when hot add the butter or margarine. Prick the duck skin all over with a sharp fork and brown the duck on all sides in the butter or oil. Transfer the duck to a saucepan or flameproof casserole.

Pour over the stock, cover and simmer over medium heat for about 1 hour 40 minutes, or until the duck is tender.

Meanwhile, heat the water and sugar together slowly in a small, heavy-based saucepan until the sugar dissolves.

Once the sugar is dissolved, turn up the heat and allow the syrup to boil rapidly until it caramelizes. Remove from the heat and pour in the vinegar or lemon juice. It will splutter. Add several spoonfulls of the cooking oil from the duck and set the caramel over medium heat. Allow mixture to come to the boil, stirring constantly.

When the duck is tender, remove it to a heated serving dish. Skim off the fat from the cooking liquid and discard. Mix the water and cornstarch together and add several spoonfulls of the duck cooking liquid. Return to the rest of the liquid and bring to the boil. Add the capers and stir over high heat until the sauce clears and thickens. Add the caramel and stir until the sauce is thick.

Cut the duck into portions or serve whole and spoon over some of the sauce. Serve the rest of the sauce separately.

SERVES 4

CHICKEN IN MUSTARD AND BRANDY SAUCE

Rich and delicious, this is a real dinner party dazzler! Your guests will appreciate your efforts, and only you will know how little time it takes to prepare.

PREPARATION TIME: 25 minutes

COOKING TIME: 30 minutes

---

8 chicken portions	2 tbsps brandy
1oz butter	2 tsps Dijon mustard
5 large garlic cloves, unpeeled	1 heaped tsp tomato purée
5 tbsps wine vinegar	½ pint double cream
½ pint dry white wine	2 tomatoes, skinned and de-seeded

Heat the butter in a large, heavy-based saucepan or frying pan. Fry the chicken thighs on both sides to brown them evenly. Add the unpeeled garlic cloves and reduce the heat.

Cover the pan and cook gently for 20 minutes, or until the chicken is tender.

Pour out all but one tablespoon of fat from the pan and add the vinegar, stirring well and scraping up any sediment from the bottom.

Boil rapidly until the liquid is reduced to about two tablespoons.

Lift out the chicken and keep warm.

Add the wine, brandy, mustard and tomato purée to the pan. Mix well and boil rapidly once again until reduced to a thick sauce (about 5 minutes).

In another heavy saucepan, boil the cream until reduced by half, stirring frequently to prevent it burning. Take off the heat.

Sieve the vinegar sauce into the cream, pressing the garlic cloves well to remove the pulp. Season with salt and black pepper.

Cut the de-seeded tomatoes into thin strips and stir into the sauce. Reheat the sauce if necessary.

Arrange the chicken on a hot serving dish and spoon over the sauce to serve.

Overleaf: Kluane Lake, Yukon. This wild and spectacular region is home to a large variety of animals, which manage to survive in one of Canada's most isolated and harshest regions.

CHAPTER
6
Family Favorites

SERVES 6

CHICKEN POT PIE

Not a true pie, this "poule-au-pot" is nevertheless welcome and warming winter fare with its creamy sauce and puffy biscuit topping. Prepare the chicken in advance, then top with the biscuit mixture at the last moment. So nice to come home to!

PREPARATION TIME: 25 minutes

COOKING TIME: 45 minutes

4 chicken joints, 2 breasts and 2 legs	6 tbsps frozen corn kernels
5 cups water	½ cup heavy cream
1 bay leaf	Salt
2 sprigs thyme	
1 sprig rosemary	**BISCUIT TOPPING**
1 sprig fresh tarragon or ¼ tsp dry tarragon	3½ cups all-purpose flour
	1½ tbsps baking powder
4 whole peppercorns	Pinch salt
1 allspice berry	5 tbsps butter or margarine
4 tbsps white wine	1½ cups milk
2 carrots, peeled and diced	1 egg, beaten with a pinch of salt
24 pearl onions, peeled	

Place the chicken in a deep saucepan with water, herbs and spices and wine. Cover and bring to the boil. Reduce the heat and allow to simmer for 20-30 minutes, or until the chicken is tender. Remove the chicken from the pot and allow to cool. Skim and discard the fat from the surface of the stock. Skin the chicken and remove the meat from the bones.

Continue to simmer the stock until reduced by about half. Strain the stock and add the carrots and onions. Cook until tender and add the corn. Stir in the cream and add the chicken. Pour into a casserole or into individual baking dishes.

To prepare the topping, sift the dry ingredients into a bowl or place them in a food processor and process once or twice to sift.

Rub in the butter or margarine until the mixture resembles small peas. Stir in enough of the milk until the mixture comes together.

Turn out onto a floured surface and knead lightly. Roll out with a floured rolling pin and cut with a pastry cutter. Brush the surface of each biscuit with a mixture of egg and salt. Place the biscuits on top of the chicken mixture and bake for 10-15 minutes in a pre-heated oven at 375°F. Serve immediately.

Below: the statue of Samuel de Champlain in Nepean Park, Ottawa.

SERVES 4

DOWN HOME BOILED DINNER

As popular in the western provinces as it is in the east, this meal-in-a-pot was brought to Nova Scotia from New England. "Corning beef" was a necessary and useful preserving process in early Canada, and fortunately we can enjoy its great flavor by buying our beef already corned.

PREPARATION TIME: 30 minutes

COOKING TIME: 3 hours

3lb corned beef brisket
1 bay leaf
1 tsp mustard seed
3 allspice berries
3 cloves
1 tsp dill seed
6 black peppercorns
2 potatoes, cut into even-sized
   pieces

4 small onions, peeled
4 large carrots, scraped
4 small or 2 large parsnips, peeled
   and cut into even-sized pieces
1 large or 2 small rutabagas
1 medium-size green cabbage, cored
   and quartered
Salt

Place the corned beef in a large saucepan with enough water to cover and add the bay leaf and spices. Cook for about 2 hours, skimming any foam from the surface as the meat cooks.

Add the potatoes and onions and cook for about 15 minutes. Taste and add salt if necessary.

Add the carrots, parsnips and rutabagas and cook for a further 15 minutes. Add the cabbage and cook a further 15 minutes.

Remove the meat from the casserole and slice it thinly. Arrange on a warm serving platter and remove the vegetables from the broth with a draining spoon, placing them around the meat. Serve immediately with horseradish or mustard.

The A. Murray Mackay Bridge links Halifax with Dartmouth in Nova Scotia.

Facing page: Fort
Edmonton Park,
Alberta, is a
reconstruction of an
1846 fur trading
post.

SERVES 4-6

BARBECUED SPARE RIBS

*A perennial backyard favorite, perked up with a dash of Chinese
spice. Bake in advance, then finish off on the outdoor grill for added
flavor!*

PREPARATION TIME: 45 minutes plus 4 hours soaking and 1 hour marinating

COOKING TIME: 1 hour

4lbs fresh spare-ribs
3 tbsps dark soy sauce
6 tbsps hoisin sauce (Chinese
    barbecue sauce)
2 tbsps dry sherry

¼ tsp five spice powder (available in
    Chinese grocers or speciality
    shops)
1 tbsp brown sugar
4-6 green onions for garnish

First prepare the garnish. Trim the root ends and the dark green tops from
the onions.

Cut both ends into thin strips, leaving about ½ inch in the middle uncut.

Place the onions in ice water for several hours or overnight for the ends to
curl up.

Cut the spare-ribs into one-rib pieces. Mix all the remaining ingredients
together, pour over the ribs and stir to coat evenly. Allow to stand for 1 hour.

Put the spare-rib pieces on a rack in a roasting pan containing 2 cups
water and cook in a preheated 350°F oven for 30 minutes. Add more hot
water to the pan while cooking, if necessary.

Turn the ribs over and brush with the remaining sauce. Cook 30 minutes
longer, or until tender. Serve garnished with the onion brushes.

Quidi Vidi is a charming Newfoundland fishing community set on a inlet so narrow that only the smallest fishing boats can be admitted.

A TRIO OF ITALIAN FAVORITES

These are lightened and lively versions of three Italian-Canadian family classics, prepared in the tradition of the finest Italian cooking. These pasta dishes are enhanced by using the freshly made pasta now readily available in food shops today, or you might like to make your own. Whichever method you choose, accompany each dish simply with a crisp green, and a glass of hearty red wine and get ready for unexpected guests!

SERVES 4

SPINACH-STUFFED CANNELLONI

Mozzarella, cheese, ham and spinach combine to make a colorful and absolutely delicious filling for cannelloni

PREPARATION TIME: 25 minutes

COOKING TIME: 35 minutes

---

12 cannelloni
8oz spinach, washed and finely
   shredded
3 slices ham, cut into thin strips
8oz Mozzarella cheese, cut into small
   cubes

1 cup white sauce
2 tbsps butter
3 tbsps grated Parmesan cheese
Pinch nutmeg
Salt and pepper

Cook the cannelloni in salted boiling water, removing them when they are still quite firm (approximately 3 minutes). Rinse them in hot water and set aside to drain on a slightly damp tea towel.

Heat the butter in a frying pan and gently cook the spinach and the ham for 2 minutes.

Remove from the heat and stir in the Mozzarella cheese.

Fill each of the cannelloni with the above stuffing.

Lay the cannelloni in a lightly-greased ovenproof dish, pour over the white sauce and season with the nutmeg, salt and pepper. Sprinkle over the Parmesan cheese and cook in a hot oven for 15 minutes. Serve piping hot.

SERVES 4

FRESH PASTA WITH BOLOGNESE SAUCE

A rich meaty sauce, cooked with white wine, carrots, onion and tomatoes.

PREPARATION TIME: 15 minutes

COOKING TIME: 50 minutes

2½ cups fresh pasta shells
1 carrot, cut into very small dice
1 onion, cut into small dice
3 cups ground beef
½ cup white wine
3 tomatoes, peeled, seeded and
  chopped

1 bay leaf
2 tbsps olive oil
¼ cup butter
½ cup water
Salt and pepper

Heat the olive oil in a casserole and fry the carrot and onion until nicely browned.

Pour in the white wine and cook until the wine has completely evaporated.

Add the ground beef to the casserole and cook for 2 minutes, stirring well.

Add the water, tomatoes and bay leaf to the casserole. Season with salt and pepper, stir well and cook over a gentle heat for a further 30 minutes.

When cooking time for the sauce is almost up. set the pasta shells to cook in a pan of salted, boiling water. Rinse the pasta and allow it to drain.

Melt the butter and stir it into the pasta shells, then pour over the sauce and serve immediately. Serve piping hot.

Facing page: Kings Landing Historical Settlement in New Brunswick contains many beautiful old buildings, including this water-powered sawmill.

SERVES 4

LASAGNE

Homemade pasta layered with a reduced wine sauce of beef, mushrooms and tomatoes make an everyday dish absolutely divine. If you're pressed, save time by using ready made pasta.

PREPARATION TIME: 45 minutes

COOKING TIME: 50 minutes

PASTA
3½ cups all-purpose flour, sifted
3 eggs, beaten
Salt

LASAGNE FILLING
1⅓lbs ground beef
1 medium onion, chopped
1 clove garlic, chopped
2 cups chicken stock

2 large mushrooms, rinsed and
    chopped
¼ cup white wine
¼ cup butter
1 tbsp tomato paste
Sprig thyme
1 bay leaf
Salt and pepper
4 tbsps grated Parmesan cheese

Make the dough by mixing together the flour, eggs and salt. Form into a ball, coat with a little flour and place in the refrigerator for 30 minutes.

Heat half of the butter in a frying pan and cook the onion and garlic until light brown.

Stir in the meat and mushrooms and cook for 2 minutes.

Deglaze the pan with the white wine, allow it to reduce and stir in 1 cup chicken stock. Add the thyme, bay leaf and tomato paste, season with salt and pepper and cook until the liquid has reduced by half. Remove the thyme and bay leaf.

Roll the dough out thinly or pass it through a pasta machine and cut into even-sized rectangular strips.

Cook the pasta strips for 1 minute in salted, boiling water, rinse under hot water and set aside to drain on a slightly damp tea towel.

Grease an ovenproof dish with the remaining butter and lay strips of pasta into the base.

Cover each layer of pasta with a layer of the meat sauce and continue layering until all the pasta and sauce has been used up.

Pour over the remaining chicken stock, sprinkle over the grated Parmesan cheese and cook in a moderately hot oven until the juices have almost entirely evaporated – approximately 40 minutes. Serve piping hot from the oven.

Above: the magnificent scenery around Lake Lillooet, British Columbia.

SERVES 6-8

SUNDAY POT ROAST

Few can forget the rich aroma which filled the house when the Sunday pot roast was left to simmer. Revive that memory and prepare an old fashioned Sunday supper for family and friends. This is an excellent method for using economical cuts of beef.

PREPARATION TIME: 30 minutes

COOKING TIME: 2-2½ hours

3lb beef roast (rump, chuck, round or top end)
Flour seasoned with salt and pepper
2 tbsps butter or margarine
1 onion stuck with 2 cloves
1 bay leaf
2 tsps fresh thyme or 1 tsp dried thyme
1 cup beef stock

4 carrots
12 small onions, peeled
4 small turnips, peeled and left whole
2 potatoes, cut into even-sized pieces
2 tbsps butter or margarine mixed with 2 tbsps flour

Dredge the beef with the seasoned flour, patting off the excess.

Melt the butter in a large, heavy-based casserole or saucepan and, when foaming, brown the meat on all sides, turning it with wooden spoons or a spatula.

When well browned, add the onion stuck with the cloves, bay leaf and thyme and pour on the stock. Cover the pan, reduce the heat and cook on top of the stove or in a pre-heated 300°F oven. Cook slowly for about 2 hours, adding more liquid, either stock or water, as necessary.

Test the meat and, if beginning to feel tender, add the vegetables. Cover and continue to cook until the meat is completely tender and the vegetables are cooked through.

Remove the meat and vegetables from the casserole or pan and place them on a warm serving platter. Skim the excess fat from the top of the sauce and bring it back to the boil.

Mix the butter and flour (beurre manie) to a smooth paste. Add about 1 tsp of the mixture to the boiling sauce and whisk thoroughly. Continue adding the mixture until the sauce is of the desired thickness. Carve the meat and spoon over some of the sauce. Serve the rest of the sauce separately.

SERVES 4

HERBY PICNIC CHICKEN

Crisp, crunchy and touched with the tang of lemon and fresh herbs, these little drumsticks make perfectly portable picnic fare. Bring plenty of French bread, the makings for salad, and a flask of cool lemonade to wash it all down. Summer perfection!

PREPARATION TIME: 25 minutes

COOKING TIME: 30-40 minutes

8 chicken drumsticks, skinned
6oz fresh white breadcrumbs
2 tbsps chopped parsley
2 tbsps chopped tarragon
Zest of 1 lemon
Salt and freshly ground black pepper
1 tbsp Dijon mustard
2oz butter
Flour for dusting
1 egg, beaten

FOR THE LEMON AND HERB BUTTER
4oz butter
Zest of ½ lemon
Squeeze lemon juice
½ tbsp chopped parsley
½ tbsp chopped tarragon

Put the breadcrumbs in a large, shallow bowl and add the parsley, tarragon and lemon zest. Season with salt and pepper and mix well.

Put the mustard and butter together in a saucepan and melt. Remove from the heat and add the breadcrumb mixture, stirring well to coat all the breadcrumbs in butter. Cool.

Heat the oven to 400°F.

Dust each drumstick with flour.

Dip into the beaten egg and then roll in the breadcrumbs, pressing the mixture on gently to give an even coating.

Lay the drumsticks on a rack over a roasting tin and bake for 30-40 minutes, or until golden and crisp. Serve with lemon and herb butter.

SERVES 4

GOLDEN FRIED CHICKEN

Everybody's favorite "once in a while" treat, this is crispy fried chicken at its classical best.

PREPARATION TIME: 20 minutes

COOKING TIME: 24 minutes

3lb frying chicken portions
2 eggs
2 cups flour
1 tsp each salt, paprika and sage

½ tsp black pepper
Pinch cayenne pepper (optional)
Oil for frying
Parsley or watercress

Rinse chicken and pat dry.

Beat the eggs in a large bowl and add the chicken one piece at a time, turning to coat.

Mix flour and seasonings in a large paper or plastic bag.

Place chicken pieces coated with egg into the bag one at a time, close bag tightly and shake to coat each piece of chicken. Alternatively, dip each coated chicken piece in a bowl of seasoned flour, shaking off the excess.

Heat oil in a large frying pan to the depth of about ½ inch.

When the oil is hot, add the chicken skin side down first. Fry about 12 minutes and then turn over. Fry a further 12 minutes or until the juices run clear.

Drain the chicken on paper towels and serve immediately. Garnish serving plate with parsley or watercress.

Below: Golden Fried Chicken.

SERVES 4-6

MOUSSAKA

There are many different recipes for this popular casserole of Greek descent. This one is light, with no potatoes and a heavenly souffle-like topping.

PREPARATION TIME: 30 minutes

COOKING TIME: 45 minutes-1 hour

---

2 large eggplant, thinly sliced
Oil for frying
2 tbsps butter or margarine
2 onions, thinly sliced
1 clove garlic, crushed
1lb ground lamb
14oz canned tomatoes
2 tbsps tomato paste
Salt and pepper
2 tsps chopped oregano
¼ tsp ground cinnamon
¼ tsp ground cumin

WHITE SAUCE
4 tbsps butter or margarine
4 tbsps flour
2 cups milk
Salt and pepper
2 tbsps grated cheese
2 eggs, separated

TOPPING
4 tbsps finely grated cheese
4 tbsps dry breadcrumbs

Preheat the oven to 350°F. Heat the oil in a large frying pan and fry the eggplant slices for about 3 minutes. Remove them and drain on paper towels.

Pour the oil from the pan and melt the butter or margarine. Fry the onion and garlic for about 4 minutes, or until golden brown. Add the lamb and cook for about 10 minutes, breaking up well with a fork. Add the tomatoes and their juice, tomato paste, oregano, spices, salt and pepper. Bring to the boil, cover the pan and allow to simmer over gentle heat for 20 minutes.

To prepare the white sauce, melt the butter in a deep saucepan and stir in the flour off the heat. Gradually pour in the milk and add a pinch of salt and pepper. Whisk or beat well and return the pan to the heat. Cook over moderate heat, stirring continuously until thickened. Add the cheese and allow the sauce to cool slightly. Beat the egg yolks with one spoonful of the hot sauce and then gradually add to the sauce.

Whip the egg whites until stiff peaks form and fold a spoonful into the hot sauce mixture. Make sure it is thoroughly incorporated and then gently fold in the remaining egg whites.

Layer the meat mixture and the eggplant slices in an ovenproof casserole, ending with a layer of eggplant. Spoon the white sauce on top and sprinkle on the topping of cheese and breadcrumbs. Cook for about 45 minutes to 1 hour or until the topping has risen slightly and formed a golden crust on top. Allow to stand for about 5 minutes before serving to make cutting easier.

SERVES 8-10

CABBAGE ROLLS

These tasty little packages offer just a hint of the rich heritage of cooking brought to our shores by the Polish immigrants. A delicious and inexpensive supper dish with you can improvise to include your own favorite fillings.

PREPARATION TIME: 30 minutes

COOKING TIME: 1-1¼ hours

---

1 head white cabbage or 2 heads
    green cabbage
6oz rice
4 tbsps butter or margarine
1 large onion, chopped
10oz ground pork, veal or beef
Salt and pepper
1 egg

SAUCE
2 tbsps butter or margarine
2 tbsps flour

2lbs canned tomatoes
1 clove garlic, crushed
½ cup chicken stock
1 tsp chopped fresh thyme or ½ tsp
    dried thyme
Pinch sugar
Salt and pepper
2 tbsps tomato paste
4 tbsps chopped parsley

Cut the core out of the cabbage completely. Place cabbage in boiling salted water and cook for 15-20 minutes for green cabbage and 25-30 minutes for white cabbage. Remove and drain in a colander or on paper towels and leave to cool.

Cook the rice in boiling salted water for about 10 minutes or until almost tender. Drain and rinse under hot water to remove the starch. Leave in a colander and make five or six wells with the handle of a wooden spoon to allow the rice to drain thoroughly. Leave to dry.

Melt 4 tbsps butter or margarine in a large frying pan and cook the onion for about 3 minutes, or until slightly softened. Add the meat and cook slowly just until the meat loses its pink color. Break the meat up with a fork as it cooks. Add salt, pepper, rice and egg and set aside to cool.

Separate the cabbage leaves and trim down the spines with a small, sharp knife. Place all the leaves out on a clean work surface and divide the filling evenly among all the leaves.

To roll up, fold in the sides around the filling and roll up from the thick end to the thin end.

Place all the cabbage rolls in a tightly fitting casserole. It may be necessary to have two layers of rolls and possibly three. Pour water into the casserole to come about half way up the rolls. Cover the casserole tightly and cook in a pre-heated 375°F oven for 30 minutes.

To prepare the sauce, put 2 tbsps butter or margarine in a heavy-based pan and stir in the flour. Cook for 1-2 minutes and add all the remaining ingredients except the chopped parsley. Bring to the boil, stirring continuously. Partially cover the pan and cook for 20 minutes over low heat. Break up the tomatoes with a fork as the sauce cooks.

Check the level of liquid in the casserole. Pour away all but ½ cup. Pour on the tomato sauce and cook, uncovered, for a further 20 minutes, or until the cabbage is tender. Sprinkle with chopped parsley before serving.

Hoodoos, strange rock formations sculpted by wind and rain, are a feature of the Valley of the Dinosaurs near Drumheller, Alberta.

Auyuittuq National Park in the Northwest Territories is an area of year-round ice and gusting winds, but it is also a land of spectacular beauty.

SERVES 4

CHILI CON CARNE

Although this dish was originally Mexican, the recipe has evolved as its popularity has grown. The version that everybody loves best is really more North American now!

PREPARATION TIME: 15 minutes

COOKING TIME: 40 minutes

1 tbsp oil	¼ tsp garlic powder
1lb ground beef	2 tbsps flour
2 tsps ground cumin	1lb canned tomatoes
2 tsps mild or hot chili powder	1lb canned red kidney beans
Pinch oregano	Chopped avocado to garnish
Salt, pepper and pinch sugar	(optional)

Heat the oil in a large saucepan and brown the meat, breaking it up with a fork as it cooks. Sprinkle on the cumin, chili powder, oregano, salt, pepper, sugar, garlic and flour. Cook, stirring frequently, over medium heat for about 3 minutes.

Add the tomatoes and their liquid and simmer 25-30 minutes.

Drain the kidney beans and add just before serving. Heat through about 5 minutes.

Garnish with chopped avocado if desired.

Canada has a rich variety of wildflowers which thrive in habitats as diverse as the tundra of the north and the sylvan forests of the south.

THE BREAD BASKET

Few things will evoke memories of home cooking better than the aroma of biscuits baking in the oven. Included here are the indispensable items on the family "comfort food" list: hot buttermilk biscuits, cornmeal muffins and a spicy fruit-nut bread. Wrap in a napkin and send to the table in a basket, then let everyone help themselves!

MAKES 6-8

BUTTERMILK BISCUITS

Best served hot with butter, these versatile biscuits go beautifully with Golden Fried Chicken or Maple Glazed Ham. You can also sweeten them with jam for breakfast, or use as a substitute for the shortcake in the Strawberry Shortcake recipe.

PREPARATION TIME: 20 minutes

COOKING TIME: 10-12 minutes

1¾ cups all-purpose flour	½ tsp baking soda
½ tsp salt	5 tbsps margarine or 4 tbsps
2 tsps baking powder	shortening
1 tsp sugar	¾ cup buttermilk

Sift the flour, salt, baking powder, sugar and baking soda into a large bowl.
Rub in the fat until the mixture resembles coarse crumbs.
Mix in enough buttermilk to form a soft dough. It may not be necessary to use all the milk.
Turn the dough out onto a floured surface and knead lightly until smooth.
Roll the dough out on a floured surface to a thickness of ½-¾ inch. Cut into rounds with a 2½ inch cookie cutter.
Place the circles of dough on a lightly-greased baking sheet about 1 inch apart. Bake in a pre-heated 450°F oven for 10-12 minutes. Serve hot.

Riding Mountain National Park, Manitoba, provides a wealth of stunning scenery in perfect riding country.

MAKES 1 LOAF

SPICED CRANBERRY NUT BREAD

Sassamanesh was the colorful Indian name for this equally colorful berry. Here, it brightens up a quickly prepared bread.

PREPARATION TIME: 25 minutes

COOKING TIME: 1 hour

2 cups all-purpose flour	½ cup orange juice
1 tsp baking powder	2 tbsps butter or margarine, melted
1 cup sugar	4 tbsps water
1 tsp baking soda	1 egg
Pinch salt	1 cup fresh cranberries, roughly
¼ tsp ground nutmeg	chopped
¼ tsp ground ginger	1 cup hazelnuts, roughly chopped

Sift the dry ingredients and spices into a large mixing bowl. Make a well in the center of the dry ingredients and pour in the orange juice, melted butter or margarine, water and egg. Using a wooden spoon, beat the liquid mixture, gradually drawing in the flour from the outside edge.

Add the cranberries and nuts and stir to mix completely.

Lightly grease a loaf pan about 9 x 5 inches. Press a strip of wax paper on the base and up the sides. Lightly grease the paper and flour the whole inside of the pan. Spoon or pour in the bread mixture and bake in a pre-heated 325°F oven for about 1 hour, or until a skewer inserted into the center of the loaf comes out clean.

Remove from the pan, carefully peel off the paper and cool on a wire rack. Lightly dust with confectioner's sugar, if desired, and cut into slices to serve.

Above: Rogers Pass and the Hermit Range in Glacier National Park, British Columbia. Overleaf: visitors come from all over the world to see Quebec's glorious fall colors

MAKES 4 CUPS

HOT PEPPER RELISH

The tradition of "putting by" was practised by the early settlers as a necessary means of spreading the bounty of the fields throughout the year. We still welcome the sight of this colorful relish at a winter's meal, bringing with it memories of bright summer days.

PREPARATION TIME: 30 minutes

COOKING TIME: 45 minutes

3lbs sweet peppers (even numbers of red, green, yellow and orange, or as available), seeded	½ tsp ground coriander
	2 bay leaves
	Salt to taste
4-6 red or green chilies, seeded and finely chopped	2 cups granulated or preserving sugar
2 medium onions, finely chopped	1½ cups white wine vinegar or white distilled vinegar
½ tsp oregano	

Cut the peppers into small dice and combine with the chilies and onions in a large saucepan.

Pour over boiling water to cover, and return to the boil. Cook rapidly for 10 minutes and drain well.

Meanwhile, combine the sugar and vinegar in a large saucepan. Bring slowly to the boil to dissolve the sugar, stirring occasionally.

When the peppers and onions have drained, add them and the remaining ingredients to the vinegar and sugar. Bring back to the boil and then simmer for 30 minutes. Remove the bay leaves and pour into sterilized jars and seal.

CHAPTER
7
Vegetables and Salads

Facing page:
completed in 1909,
Winnipeg's
Legislative Building
is a beautiful
example of the Neo-
Classical style.

SERVES 6

SUCCOTASH

A very old recipe inherited (along with its name) from the Indians which has remained a popular side dish simply because of its healthy goodness and fresh taste. Try it using summer's first sweetcorn and see!

PREPARATION TIME: 10 minutes for frozen vegetables
25 minutes for fresh vegetables

COOKING TIME: 5-8 minutes for frozen vegetables
8-10 minutes for fresh vegetables

4oz fresh or frozen corn	3 tbsps butter
4oz fresh or frozen lima beans	Salt and pepper
4oz fresh or frozen green beans	Chopped parsley

If using frozen vegetables, bring water to the boil in a saucepan and, when boiling, add the vegetables. Cook for about 5-8 minutes, drain and leave to dry.

If using fresh vegetables, bring water to the boil in a saucepan and add the lima beans first. After about 2 minutes, add the green beans. Follow these with the corn about 3 minutes before the end of cooking time. Drain and leave to dry.

Melt the butter in a saucepan and add the vegetables. Heat slowly, tossing or stirring occasionally, until heated through. Add salt and pepper to taste and stir in the parsley. Serve immediately.

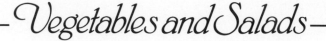

SERVES 4

TOMATO AND ORANGE SALAD WITH MOZZARELLA AND BASIL

Sunny West Coast flair exerts its influence on this famous Italian salad of juicy ripe tomatoes and fresh mozzarella cheese.

PREPARATION TIME: 20-25 minutes

4 large tomatoes
4 small oranges
8oz mozzarella cheese
8 fresh basil leaves

4 tbsps olive oil
1 tbsp balsamic vinegar
Salt and pepper

Remove the cores from the tomatoes and slice into rounds about ¼ inch thick.

Cut a slice from the top and bottom of each orange and, using a serrated fruit knife, remove the peel in thin strips. Make sure to cut off all the white pith. Slice oranges into ¼ inch thick rounds. Slice the mozzarella cheese into the same thickness.

Arrange the tomatoes, oranges and mozzarella in overlapping circles, alternating each ingredient.

Use scissors to shred the basil leaves finely, and sprinkle over the salad.

Mix the remaining ingredients together well and spoon over the salad. Chill briefly before serving.

Right: the cliffs and beach at Rocky Bay, Cape Breton Highlands

SERVES 6

WALNUT CRUNCH SALAD

Walnuts add a nutty crunch to this colorful variation of coleslaw.

PREPARATION TIME: 23-30 minutes

1 small head red cabbage	6 tbsps oil
1 avocado, peeled and cubed	2 tbsps white wine vinegar
1 carrot, grated	2 tsps dry mustard
4 green onions, shredded	Salt and pepper
1 cup chopped walnuts	

Cut the cabbage in quarters and remove the core. Use a large knife to shred finely or use the thick slicing blade on a food processor.

To cube the avocado, first cut in half lengthwise and twist to separate. Tap the stone sharply with a knife and twist to remove. Place the avocado halves cut side down, score the skin with a sharp knife and then peel the strips of skin backward to remove them. Cut into strips and then crosswise into cubes.

Combine the cabbage, avocado and shredded carrot with the onions and walnuts in a large bowl.

Mix the remaining ingredients together well and pour over the salad. Toss carefully to avoid breaking up the avocado. Chill before serving.

SERVES 4-6

MARINATED MUSHROOM SALAD

*Try adding some wild (dried or fresh) mushrooms to this
wonderfully woodsy salad.*

PREPARATION TIME: 10 minutes plus 1-2 hours for marinating

1lb mushrooms
1 medium onion
3 tbsps oil
1 tbsp chopped parsley
1 dill pickle, diced

3-4 tomatoes, peeled, seeded and
    diced
4 tbsps oil
1 tbsp wine vinegar
Salt and pepper
Pinch sugar

Slice the mushrooms thinly and chop the onion finely. Heat 3 tbsps oil in a
large sauté pan and add the mushrooms and onions. Cook for about 2-3
minutes to soften slightly. Remove from the heat and allow to cool.

    When the mushrooms and onions have completely cooled, add the
parsley, dill pickle and tomatoes. Mix together the oil and vinegar, sugar and
salt and pepper and pour over the other ingredients. Stir gently to coat evenly
and allow to stand for 1-2 hours in the refrigerator before serving.

SERVES 4

ACORN SQUASH WITH BLUEBERRIES

A self-contained autumn vegetable dish filled with sweet berries and apples, so pretty it need only be served with simply cooked poultry or meat. Try it on its own for a light vegetarian meal.

PREPARATION TIME: 30 minutes

COOKING TIME: 50-55 minutes

Above: yachts bask in a quiet sunset over the Burrard Inlet, Vancouver. Overleaf: the Legislative Building in Regina, Saskatchewan.

2 acorn squash	Freshly grated nutmeg
1 small apple, peeled and chopped	4 tbsps butter or margarine
4 tbsps light brown sugar	6oz fresh or frozen blueberries

Cut the squash in half lengthwise. Scoop out the seeds and discard them.
   Fill the hollows with the chopped apple.
   Sprinkle on the sugar and nutmeg and dot with the butter or margarine.
   Place the squash in a baking dish and pour in about 1 inch of water. Bake, covered, for 40-45 minutes at 375°F. Uncover, add the blueberries and cook an additional 10 minutes.

SERVES 4

CHEESE STUFFED TOMATOES

Use summer's ripe tomatoes to showcase this creamy and appetizing filling for starters. Alternatively hollow out some tiny cherry tomatoes, stuff and pass on a colorful hors d'oeuvres platter before the meal.

PREPARATION TIME: 15 minutes plus 30 minutes for the tomatoes to chill

4 beefsteak tomatoes	4 anchovy fillets
4oz Canadian Camembert or French Brie	1 tbsp capers
	2 tsps caraway seeds
2 green onions	Salt and freshly ground black pepper

Remove the core from the bottom of each tomato. Cut a slice from the rounded end of each tomato and scoop out the pulp and seeds with a small teaspoon. Strain out the seeds and use the pulp and juice for the filling.

Place the anchovies in a little milk and leave to soak for about 5 minutes. Rinse, pat dry and chop. If the capers are large, chop them roughly. Chop the green onions finely and mash with the cheese, capers, anchovies, caraway seeds, salt and pepper. Add the reserved tomato juice and pulp and mix the ingredients together thoroughly.

Spoon the filling into the tomatoes and place them on serving plates. Top with the reserved tomato slices and serve chilled.

SERVES 6

ZUCCHINI SLIPPERS

It would be hard to imagine our vegetable gardens without this prolific plant, but it was the Italian immigrants who popularized the zucchini and showed us so many wonderful ways with this squash. Now its time to share the wealth!

PREPARATION TIME: 30 minutes

COOKING TIME: 23-25 minutes

6 even-sized zucchini	2 tbsps chopped parsley
4oz cottage cheese, drained	Pinch salt and cayenne pepper
4oz grated Cheddar cheese	1 large egg
1 small red pepper, seeded and chopped	Watercress or parsley to garnish

Trim the ends of the zucchini and cook in boiling salted water for about 8 minutes, or steam for 10 minutes.

Remove from the water or steamer and cut in half. Allow to cool slightly and then scoop out the center, leaving a narrow margin of flesh on the skin to form a shell. Invert each zucchini slipper onto a paper towel to drain, reserving the scooped-out flesh.

Chop the flesh and mix with the remaining ingredients.

Spoon filling into the shells and arrange in a greased baking dish. Bake, uncovered, in a pre-heated 350°F oven for 15 minutes. Broil, if desired, to brown the top. Garnish with watercress or parsley.

Ellesmere Island, with its glaciers, valleys and fiords, is one of Canada's most remote and spectacular parks.

SERVES 6

CREAMY SCALLOPED POTATOES

Far from common fare, this dish elevates the potato to a rich and flavorful accompaniment to poultry, roast meats and especially ham.

1 clove garlic, peeled and crushed with the flat of a knife	½ cup light cream
2 tbsps butter	Salt and pepper
2¼lbs potatoes, peeled and thinly sliced	1½ cups grated Cheddar or Gruyère cheese
	⅓ cup butter cut into very small dice

Preheat the oven to 400°F. Rub the bottom and sides of a heavy baking dish with the crushed clove of garlic. Grease the bottom and sides liberally with the butter. Use a dish that can also be employed as a serving dish.

Spread half of the potato slices in the bottom of the dish, sprinkle with cheese, salt and pepper and dot with the butter dice. Top with the remaining slices of potato neatly arranged. Sprinkle with the remaining cheese, salt, pepper and butter.

Pour the cream into the side of the dish around the potatoes.

Cook in the top part of the oven for 30-40 minutes, or until the potatoes are tender and the top is nicely browned. Serve immediately.

SERVES 4-6

MINTED MIXED VEGETABLES

A light and popular side dish of carrots, cucumber and zucchini, all complemented by the tang of fresh mint. You can use this recipe to experiment with your own combinations, using the freshest vegetables in season.

PREPARATION TIME: 25-30 minutes

COOKING TIME: 6-10 minutes

3 medium carrots	Pinch salt
1 cucumber	1½ tbsps butter, cut into small pieces
2 zucchini	1 tbsp coarsely chopped fresh mint
½ cup water	leaves
1 tsp sugar	

The colors of fall in Quebec have been an inspiration to countless writers and artists as well as to the large numbers of visitors who come to the region to witness the autumn display.

Peel the carrots and cut them into sticks about ½ inch thick and 2½ inches long.

Peel the cucumber and cut it into quarters. Remove the centers and cut into sticks the same size as the carrots.

Cut the zucchini into sticks the same size as the other vegetables.

Combine the carrots, water, sugar and salt in a medium saucepan. Cover the pan and bring to the boil over high heat. Reduce the heat to medium and cook for about 3 minutes. Uncover the pan and cook a further 3 minutes.

Increase the heat and add the cucumber and zucchini and boil until the vegetables are tender crisp. Add the butter and stir over heat until melted and the liquid has completely evaporated, glazing the vegetables. Remove from the heat, add the mint and toss well.

SERVES 6

COOL CUCUMBER SALAD

Refreshing and light, this dill cucumber salad always seems heaven sent on a steamy summer's day. Serve it with new potatoes and freshly poached salmon. Delicious!

PREPARATION TIME: 30 minutes

1 large cucumber	1 tsp sugar
½ cup sour cream	1 tbsp chopped fresh dill
2 tsps white wine vinegar	Salt and pepper

Wash the cucumber well. Trim off the thin ends of the cucumber.

Using a cannelle knife or the prongs of a fork, score the skin of the cucumber in long strips.

Cut the cucumber into thin slices and place in a colander. Sprinkle with salt and leave for 30 minutes.

Place the colander in a bowl to collect the cucumber liquid. Rinse the cucumber well and pat dry.

Mix the remaining ingredients together in a large bowl and toss with the cucumber slices.

Arrange the cucumber in a serving dish and serve chilled.

SERVES 4-6

CAESAR SALAD

California couldn't contain the popularity of this now classic salad, appreciated by all who love its lemony rich crunch.

PREPARATION TIME: 30 minutes

COOKING TIME: 3-5 minutes for the croûtons

---

6 anchovy fillets, soaked in 4 tbsps milk
1 cup olive oil
1 clove garlic, left whole
4 slices French bread, cut into ½ inch cubes

1 egg, cooked 1 minute
1 head Romaine lettuce
Juice of 1 small lemon
Salt and pepper
4 tbsps grated Parmesan cheese

Leave the anchovies to soak in the milk for 15 minutes. Rinse and pat dry on paper towels. Chop roughly.

Crush the garlic and leave in the oil for about 30 minutes. Heat all but 6 tbsps of the oil in a frying pan until hot. Fry the cubes of bread until golden brown, stirring constantly with a metal spoon for even browning. Drain on paper towels.

Break the cooked egg into a bowl and beat well with the lemon juice, salt and pepper. Toss the lettuce with the remaining garlic oil and anchovies. Add the egg white mixture and toss to coat well. Place in a clean serving bowl and sprinkle over the croûtons and Parmesan cheese. Serve at room temperature.

Overleaf: the entrance to the ominously named Dead Men's Valley in Nahanni National Park, Northwest Territories.

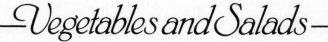

SERVES 4

VEGETABLE RIBBONS
WITH PESTO

A stylish vegetable presentation with international overtones. There is no substitute for fresh basil in the sauce, so prepare it in the summer when basil is plentiful to freeze for later.

PREPARATION TIME: 30-40 minutes

COOKING TIME: 45 minutes

2 large zucchini, ends trimmed	2 small shallots, chopped
2 medium carrots, peeled	2-3oz fresh basil leaves
1 large or 2 small leeks, trimmed, halved and well washed	1-1½ cups olive oil
1 cup shelled pistachio nuts	Salt and pepper

Left: lobster pots on the shore of the Gaspé Peninsula, a wild, wave-battered region where many communities still make their living from the sea.

Cut the zucchini and carrots into long, thin slices with a mandolin or by hand. A food processor will work but the slices will be short.

Cut the leeks into lengths the same size as the zucchini and carrots. Make sure the leeks are well rinsed in between all layers. Cut into long, thin strips.

Using a large, sharp knife, cut the zucchini and carrot slices into long, thin strips about the thickness of 2 matchsticks. The julienne blade of a food processor will produce strips that are too fine to use.

Place the carrot strips in a pan of boiling salted water and cook for about 3-4 minutes or until tender crisp. Drain and rinse under cold water. Cook the zucchini strips separately for about 2-3 minutes and add the leek strips during the last 1 minute of cooking. Drain and rinse the vegetables and leave with the carrots to drain dry.

Place the nuts, shallots and basil in the bowl of a food processor or in a blender and chop finely.

Reserve about 3 tbsps of the olive oil for later use. With the machine running, pour the remaining oil through the funnel in a thin, steady stream. Use enough oil to bring the mixture to the consistency of mayonnaise. Add seasoning to taste.

Place reserved oil in a large pan and, when hot, add the drained vegetables. Season and toss over moderate heat until heated through. Add the pesto sauce and toss gently to coat the vegetables. Serve immediately.

Facing page: beech maples form a delightful green canopy in a forest on Hill Island, one of the St. Lawrence Islands.
Overleaf: Banff National Park, with its forbidding peaks and lowland valleys, lies under a blanket of winter snow.

SERVES 6-8

HOT POTATO SALAD WITH BACON

The wilderness of Kitchener and Waterloo Counties in Ontario became home to the Mennonites when they immigrated during the 1800's. This creamy, warm salad, a legacy of those days of barn raising and sewing bees, is one of their best known and most popular.

PREPARATION TIME: 25 minutes

COOKING TIME: 35 minutes

6-8 even-sized potatoes (waxy variety)	½ cup white wine vinegar
Pinch salt	½ cup water or beef stock
4oz bacon, diced	3 tbsps sour cream (optional)
1 onion	2 tbsps chopped parsley
	Salt and pepper

Boil the potatoes in their jackets in lightly salted water to cover. When the potatoes are just tender, drain and peel while still hot. Cut into thin slices and place in a serving dish.

Fry the bacon in a large frying pan or sauté pan. While the bacon is frying, chop the onion very finely. Once the bacon is pale golden brown add the onions and continue to sauté slowly until they become transparent but not brown. Remove the pan from the heat and carefully pour in the vinegar and the water or stock. Do this gradually so that the hot fat does not spatter.

Bring to the boil and remove from the heat. Stir in the sour cream, if using, and pour the mixture over the potatoes. Lift the potatoes so that the dressing runs over them evenly. Sprinkle with salt and pepper and parsley. Serve immediately.

CHAPTER
8
Desserts and Ices

SERVES 6

STRIPED SORBET SURPRISE

This tri-colored iced sorbet bombe is bound to surprise and delight at the end of a special summer meal. It can be prepared well ahead, then garnished just before serving.

PREPARATION TIME: 35 minutes plus overnight freezing

2 cups water
1 cup sugar
Juice of 1-2 lemons
8 kiwi fruit, peeled and roughly
   chopped
4 ripe bananas, peeled and roughly
   chopped

1lb raspberries, fresh or well drained
   frozen
2 egg whites
1 banana, 1 kiwi fruit, sliced and
   whole raspberries to garnish

Combine the water and sugar in a heavy-based saucepan. Bring slowly to the boil to dissolve the sugar.

When the sugar is completely dissolved, boil the syrup rapidly for about 1 minute. Allow it to cool completely and then refrigerate until completely cold.

Purée the kiwi fruit in a food processor, sieving to remove the seeds if desired. Purée the bananas and the raspberries separately. Sieve the raspberries to remove the seeds.

Divide the cold syrup in 3 parts and mix each with one of the fruit purées. Taste each and add about 1-2 tbsps of lemon juice to each fruit syrup, depending on the sweetness of the fruit.

Freeze the fruit syrups separately until almost solid, about 2 hours, then mix again in the food processor to break up ice crystals. Freeze again separately until solid.

Whip the egg whites until stiff. Process the sorbets again, separately, dividing the egg white among all three.

Pour the raspberry sorbet into a bowl or mold and freeze until firm.

Pour the banana sorbet on top and freeze again.

Finish with the kiwi sorbet and freeze overnight or until firm.

To unmold, dip briefly in hot water and invert on a plate. Garnish with the prepared fruit.

SERVES 4

CHOCOLATE ICE CREAM

"Chocoholics" need travel no further, this is the ultimate in chocolate ice creams; smooth and rich, made from a velvety egg custard sauce.

PREPARATION TIME: 30 minutes plus about 1 hour freezing time

½ cup sugar	4 tbsps chocolate powder
6 egg yolks	(unsweetened)
2 cups milk	

Whisk the egg yolk and sugar together until the mixture whitens.

Bring the milk to boil in a large saucepan.

Whisk in the egg mixture, reduce the heat and whisk continuously until the mixture thickens.

Once the sauce is thick, remove from the heat and stir in the chocolate powder.

Pour the mixture into the bowl of an ice cream maker and set in motion.*

Once the ice cream has crystallized it can be spooned into a container and kept in the freezer until needed.

*If an ice cream maker is not available, pour the mixture into a bowl and place in the freezer until mushy. Remove bowl from freezer and whisk the mixture. Refreeze, whisk thoroughly, pour into a covered container and freeze until firm.

Facing page: the Alberta Legislative Building, Edmonton. Overleaf: a crescent moon shines over the still forests of Terra Nova National Park, Newfoundland.

SERVES 4-6

MAPLE SYRUP MOUSSE

In Eastern Canada "sugaring off" or the tapping of the maple's sweet sap begins in early spring when the sunny days and cooler nights touch off the sweet flow.
Traditionally, the clear sap was cooked down over wood smoke fires in the sugarbush, then made into syrup or hard sugar cakes to be used all year long. This was a great time for socializing, and a signal to start preparing the many traditional recipes utilizing the 'brown sweetness' as it was then called. One of the most delightful ways of enjoying this pure delicacy is in a light and silky mousse. Serve it when spring is in the air.

PREPARATION TIME: 40 minutes

4 eggs, separated	1 cup heavy cream
2 extra egg whites	Chopped pecans or walnuts to
¾ cup maple syrup	decorate

Place the syrup in a saucepan and bring to the boil. Continue boiling to reduce the syrup by one quarter.

Beat the egg yolks until thick and lemon colored.

Pour the maple syrup onto the egg yolks in a thin, steady stream, beating with an electric mixer. Continue beating until the mixture has cooled.

Beat the egg whites until stiff but not dry and whip the cream until soft peaks form.

Fold the cream and egg whites into the maple mixture and spoon into a serving bowl or individual glasses. Refrigerate until slightly set and top with chopped walnuts or pecans to serve.

Left: the pristine Stanhope Cape Lighthouse on Prince Edward Island.

Above: Victoria's
Legislative Building
and harbor by night.

MAKES 1 PIE

BLUEBERRY PIE

*Remember those prickly hot summer days picking wild blueberries?
A pie just like this was the anticipated reward for generations of
Canadians who filled their baskets.*

PREPARATION TIME: 30-40 minutes

COOKING TIME: 50-55 minutes

Double quantity pastry for Pumpkin
   Pie recipe

FILLING
1lb blueberries
2 tbsps cornstarch

4 tbsps water
2 tbsps lemon juice
1 cup sugar
1 egg beaten with a pinch of salt

Prepare the pastry in the same way as for the Pumpkin Pie recipe.

Divide the pastry in half and roll out one half to form the base. Use a floured rolling pin to lower it into the dish, and press it against the sides. Chill the pastry in the dish and the remaining half of the pastry while preparing the filling.

Place the fruit in a bowl and mix the cornstarch with the water and lemon juice. Pour it over the fruit, add the sugar and mix together gently.

Spoon the fruit filling into the pastry base.

Roll out the remaining pastry on a lightly-floured surface and cut into strips.

Use the strips to make a lattice pattern on top of the filling and press the edges to stick them to the pastry base. Cut off any excess pastry.

Using your fingers or a fork, crimp the edges to decorate.

Brush the crimped edge of the pastry and the lattice strips lightly with the beaten egg and bake in a pre-heated 425°F oven for about 10 minutes. Reduce the heat to 350°F and bake for a further 40-45 minutes. Serve warm or cold.

SERVES 8

CARAMEL CUSTARD WITH ORANGE AND CORIANDER

Depending on where one hears it, this much loved caramel cream is a classic inherited from several European cuisines. Origins notwithstanding, the addition of orange and fragrant coriander provides a brilliant blend of flavors, color and new appeal.

PREPARATION TIME: 30-40 minutes

COOKING TIME: 40 minutes

6oz sugar	1 tbsp coriander seeds, crushed
6 tbsps water	6 eggs
3 small oranges	2 egg yolks
3 cups milk	6oz sugar

To prepare the caramel, put the sugar and water in a heavy-based saucepan and bring to the boil over gentle heat to dissolve the sugar.

Once the sugar is dissolved, bring to the boil over high heat and cook to a golden brown, watching the color carefully.

While the caramel is cooking, heat 8 custard cups to warm them. When the caramel is brown, pour an equal amount into each cup and swirl quickly to coat the base and sides with caramel. Leave the caramel to cool and harden in the cups.

Grate the oranges and combine the rind, milk and crushed coriander seeds in a deep saucepan. Set the oranges aside for later use. Bring the milk almost to boiling point and set it aside for the flavors to infuse.

Beat the eggs, yolks and sugar together until light and fluffy. Gradually strain on the milk, stirring well in between each addition. Pour the milk over the caramel in each cup. Place the cups in a bain-marie and place in a preheated 325°F oven for about 40 minutes, or until a knife inserted into the center of the custards comes out clean. Lower oven temperature slightly if the water begins to boil around the cups.

When the custards are cooked, remove the cups from the bain-marie and refrigerate for at least 3 hours or overnight until the custard is completely cold and set.

To serve, loosen the custards from the sides of the cup with a small knife and turn them out onto individual plates. Peel the white pith from around the oranges and segment them. Place some of the orange segments around the custards and serve immediately

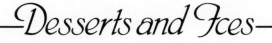

SERVES 6

MOUSSE AU CHOCOLAT

The French have been making chocolate since the mid-sixteenth century, but the New World had another century to wait before sampling this concentrated confection. Make up for lost time by indulging in this French dessert; elegant and irresistible, this is a dark chocolate mixture which sets to a rich cream when cooled.

PREPARATION TIME: 30 minutes plus overnight chilling

6oz semi-sweet chocolate	3 eggs, separated
Scant ⅓ cup water	2 tbsps rum
1 tbsp butter	

Chop the chocolate into small pieces and combine with the water in a heavy-based saucepan. Cook over very gentle heat so that the chocolate and water form a thick cream. Remove from the heat, allow to cool slightly and then beat in the butter.

Add the rum and beat in the egg yolks one at a time.

Whip the egg whites until stiff but not dry and fold thoroughly into the chocolate mixture. Pour into small pots or custard cups and chill overnight. Finish with whipped cream and chocolate curls to serve, if desired.

SERVES 4-6

BANANA ICE CREAM

A delicious ice cream that is a favorite with children – for adults, add a spoonful of rum!

PREPARATION TIME: 30 minutes plus 1 hour freezing time

FOR 4 CUPS EGG CUSTARD	½ cup sugar
4 cups milk	½lb peeled banana
12 egg yolks	Few drops lemon juice

Prepare the egg custard in the usual way. Whisk the eggs and sugar together until the mixture pales. Bring the milk to the boil and stir in the egg-sugar mixture. Reduce the heat and continue stirring until the mixture thickens. For this recipe use 1 cup of the egg custard, using the remainder for other flavored ice cream.

Mash the banana with a fork and add a few drops of lemon juice.
Add the banana to the egg custard and blend smooth with a hand mixer.
Pour into the bowl of an ice cream maker and set in motion.*
Spoon into a container and keep in the freezer until needed.
*If an ice cream maker is not available, pour the mixture into a bowl and place in the freezer until part frozen. Remove from the freezer and whisk. Refreeze and whisk thoroughly until smooth. Pour into a covered container and replace in the freezer until required.

A sinking sun lights the path of pronghorns, one of the many species that forage in Canada's wilderness areas.

SERVES 8

BREAD PUDDING WITH RUM SAUCE

A soothing childhood pudding that has been revamped with an adult sauce and a stylish presentation. The result is a rich and creamy, rum and raisin concoction that is ready to take on a whole new generation!

PREPARATION TIME: 40 minutes

COOKING TIME: 1 hour

½ loaf day-old French bread	Butter or margarine
2 cups milk	½ cup butter
3 eggs	1 cup sugar
¾ cup raisins	1 egg
1 tsp vanilla extract	4 tbsps rum or brandy
Pinch ground ginger	Nutmeg

Cut bread into small pieces and soak in the milk.

When the bread has softened, add the eggs, raisins, vanilla and ginger.

Grease 8 custard cups with butter or margarine and fill each with an equal amount of pudding mixture to within ½ inch of the top.

Place the dishes in a roasting pan and pour in enough hot water to come halfway up the sides of the dishes. Bake in a preheated 350°F oven until risen and set – about 35-40 minutes.

When the puddings have cooked, combine the ½ cup butter and the sugar in the top of a double boiler and heat to dissolve the sugar.

Beat the egg and stir in a spoonful of the hot butter mixture. Add the egg to the double boiler and whisk over heat until thick. Allow to cool and add the rum or brandy.

To serve, turn out puddings onto plates and surround with sauce. Sprinkle the tops with nutmeg.

Facing page: the frozen wastes of the Northwest Territories. Despite the desolate appearance, this vast region is home to a large number of wild animals.

MAKES 1 CAKE

SPICY GINGERBREAD CAKE

This soft and spicy cake is ever popular with young and old alike. Serve it hot with green apple sauce for an old-fashioned treat, or simply on its own with coffee, tea or with milk as a snack.

PREPARATION TIME: 20 minutes

COOKING TIME: 45 minutes

1 cup vegetable shortening	1½ tsps ground ginger
1 cup molasses	1 tsp cinnamon
3 eggs, beaten	¼ tsp ground nutmeg
3 cups all-purpose flour	Pinch ground cloves
1 tbsp baking powder	4 tbsps chopped walnuts
Pinch salt	4 tbsps raisins

Cream the shortening until light and fluffy. Add the molasses and beat with an electric mixer. Add the eggs one at a time, beating well in between each addition.

Sift the flour together with a pinch of salt and baking powder. Combine with the molasses mixture and add the spices.

Stir in the nuts and raisins and pour the mixture into a lightly greased 9×13 inch baking pan.

Bake for about 45 minutes in a pre-heated 375°F oven.

To test for doneness, insert a skewer into the center of the cake. If it comes out clean, the cake is done. Allow to cool and cut into squares to serve.

Above: a fine old church in Medicine Hat, Alberta, a town whose prosperity lies in its large reserves of natural gas.

SERVES 4

MANGO AND COCONUT WITH LIME SABAYON

A taste for the more exotic combined with modern transportation methods now allow us to enjoy the fruits of our far-flung neighbors. Here mango mingles with a creamy lime sauce to make a sensationally easy and stylish dessert.

PREPARATION TIME: 40 minutes

COOKING TIME: 8 minutes

---

2 large, ripe mangoes, peeled and
    sliced
1 fresh coconut
2 egg yolks

4 tbsps sugar
Juice and grated rind of 2 limes
½ cup heavy cream, whipped

Arrange thin slices of mango on plates.

Break coconut in half and then into smaller sections. Grate the white pulp, taking care to avoid grating the brown skin. Use the coarse side of the greater to make shreds and scatter them over the mango slices.

Place egg yolks and sugar in the top of a double boiler or a large bowl. Whisk until very thick and lemon colored.

Stir in the lime juice and place mixture over simmering water. Whisk constantly while the mixture gently cooks and becomes thick and creamy.

Remove from the heat and place in another bowl of iced water to cool quickly. Whisk the mixture while it cools.

Fold in the whipped cream and spoon onto the fruit. Garnish with the grated lime rind.

Overleaf: the sun sinks below the skyline of Toronto, Canada's largest metropolis and its main busines center.

MAKES 1 PIE

MOCHA MAGIC ICE CREAM PIE

A chocolate and coffee ice cream confection that is unbelievably simple to make, yet tastes delicious and is impressive to serve. A cooling end to a spicy meal or a lovely late-night treat.

PREPARATION TIME: 25 minutes plus several hours to freeze

8-10 Graham crackers or digestive biscuits, crushed
½ cup butter or margarine, melted
3 cups coffee ice cream

2oz semi-sweet chocolate, melted
4oz shredded coconut
Dark rum

Crush crackers with a rolling pin or in a food processor. Mix with melted butter or margarine.

Press into an 8½ inch false-bottomed flan dish. Chill thoroughly in the refrigerator.

Meanwhile, combine 4 tbsps coconut with the melted chocolate. When cooled but not solidified, add about a quarter of the coffee ice cream, mixing well.

Spread the mixture on the base of a crust and freeze until firm.

Soften the remaining ice cream with an electric mixer or food processor and spread over the chocolate-coconut layer. Re-freeze until firm.

Toast the remaining coconut in a moderate oven, stirring frequently until golden brown. Allow to cool completely.

Remove the pie from the freezer and leave in the refrigerator 30 minutes before serving. Push up the base of the dish and place the pie on a serving plate. Sprinkle the top with toasted coconut. Cut into wedges and drizzle with rum before serving.

Left: the mighty cataract of the Bakers Brook Falls in Newfoundland.

Visitors to the province cannot fail to be astounded by the beauty and variety of the wildflowers on Prince Edward Island.

SERVES 6

FROZEN LIME AND BLUEBERRY CREAM

Blueberries grow wild in many parts of Canada and recipes featuring their unique flavor continue to flourish. Here, a beautifully colored meringue cream combines the berries with the tangy tartness of the lime for a refreshingly cool and stunning sweet.

PREPARATION TIME: 40 minutes plus overnight freezing

Juice and rind of 4 limes	4oz blueberries
Water	3 egg whites
1 cup sugar	1 cup heavy cream, whipped

Measure the lime juice and make up to 6 tbsps with water if necessary.

Combine with the sugar in a heavy-based pan and bring to the boil slowly to dissolve the sugar.

When the mixture forms a clear syrup, boil rapidly to 250°F on a sugar thermometer.

Meanwhile, combine the blueberries with about 4 tbsps water in a small saucepan. Bring to the boil and then simmer, covered, until very soft. Purée, sieve to remove the seeds and skin, and set aside to cool.

Whisk the egg whites until stiff but not dry and then pour on the hot sugar syrup in a steady stream, whisking constantly. Add the lime rind and allow the meringue to cool.

When cold, fold in the whipped cream. Pour in the purée and marble through the mixture with a rubber spatula. Do not over-fold. Pour the mixture into a lightly-oiled mold or bowl and freeze until firm. Leave 30 minutes in the refrigerator before serving or dip the mold for about 10 seconds in hot water. Place a plate over the bottom of the mold, invert and shake to turn out. Garnish with extra whipped cream, blueberries or lime slices.

Facing page:
Strawberry Ice
Cream.

SERVES 4

STRAWBERRY ICE CREAM

*Who can resist summertime's great harvest, symbolised by the creamy
pink celebration of the strawberry. Left in chunks or smooth as silk,
the beautiful berry flavor is sealed into each luscious bite.
Sit back and savor!*

PREPARATION TIME: 35 minutes (including time to make the custard) plus 1 hour
freezing time

1 cup egg custard (see Banana Ice Cream recipe) ¼ cup light cream	Generous cup of strawberries, washed and hulled

Either chop the strawberries into small pieces and mix them into the egg
custard, or add them whole to the custard and blend smooth with a hand
mixer.

Stir in the cream and pour into the bowl of an ice cream maker. Set the
machine in motion*

When the ice cream has 'taken', spoon into a container and keep in the
freezer until needed.

*If an ice cream maker is not available, part freeze the mixture in a bowl,
whisk and refreeze. Whisk again, pour into a covered container and freeze
until firm.

SERVES 4

RHUBARB SORBET

*Early forced rhubarb is bright pink in color and gradually turns to
pale green as the summer progresses. Whatever the color, its fresh, tart
flavor is perfectly refreshing and makes a particularly nice sorbet. The
ideal dessert after a rich meal.*

PREPARATION TIME: 10 minutes plus 40 minutes freezing time

1½ cups water ⅞ cup sugar	1lb rhubarb

Peel the rhubarb and cut the stalks into small pieces.

Mix together in a saucepan the water, sugar and rhubarb.

Bring to the boil and cook for 5 minutes.

Blend smooth with a hand mixer and pour into the bowl of an ice cream
maker. Set the machine in motion and remove when the sorbet is crystallized.
Spoon into a container and keep in the freezer until needed.

*If an ice cream maker is not available, part freeze the mixture in a
shallow container, break up gently with a fork and then pour into a covered
container and freeze until needed.

MAKES 24-30

HAZELNUT FLORENTINES

Hazelnuts make a good alternative to almonds in these crisp, toffee like confections. Enjoy as they are with ice creams, or make into tiny bites to serve as petit fours with coffee.

PREPARATION TIME: 45-50 minutes

COOKING TIME: 10 minutes per batch

1lb shelled and peeled hazelnuts	1 cup butter
1 cup sugar	6oz white chocolate, melted
6 tbsps honey	6oz semi-sweet chocolate, melted
6 tbsps heavy cream	

Place hazelnuts in a plastic bag and tie securely. Tap nuts or roll them along with a rolling pin to crush roughly.

Place sugar, honey, cream and butter in a heavy-based saucepan and heat gently to dissolve sugar. Bring to the boil and cook rapidly for about 1½ minutes. Remove from heat and stir in the nuts.

Brush baking sheets well with oil and spoon or pour out mixture in even amounts. Make only about six Florentines at a time.

Bake about 10 minutes in a pre-heated 375°F oven. Allow to cool on the baking sheets and, when nearly set, loosen with a spatula and transfer to a flat surface to cool completely.

When all Florentines have been baked and cooled, melt both chocolates separately. Spread white chocolate on half of the Florentines and semi-sweet chocolate on the other half, or marble the two if desired.

Place chocolate side uppermost to cool slightly and then make a wavy pattern with the tines of a fork, or swirl chocolate with a knife until it sets in the desired pattern.

Shaped over the years by the sea and the elements, the coast of the Gaspé Peninsula comprises tall, craggy cliffs and long shingle beaches.

Above: the unique Thousand Islands Skydeck on Hill Island and, in the background, the Thousand Islands International Bridge, which spans the St. Lawrence River.

SERVES 6

PEARS IN SPICY WINE

Both the Bosc pears and the fragrant wines used for this luscious dessert are grown in the temperate regions of Southern Ontario and the Okanagan Valley, British Columbia. The garnish of crisp almonds simply compliments nature's perfect marriage.

PREPARATION TIME: 25 minutes

COOKING TIME: 50 minutes

3 cups Canadian dry red wine
1 cup sugar
1 cinnamon stick
1 strip lemon peel
6 Bosc pears, even sized

4 tbsps sliced almonds
1 tbsp cornstarch mixed with 3 tbsps
   water
Mint leaves to garnish

Pour the wine into a deep saucepan that will hold 6 pears standing upright.

Add the sugar, cinnamon and lemon peel, and bring to the boil slowly to dissolve the sugar. Stir occasionally.

Peel pears, remove 'eye' on the bottom, but leave on the stems.

Stand the pears close together in the wine, so that they remain standing. Cover the pan and poach gently over low heat for about 25-35 minutes, or until tender. If the wine does not cover the pears completely, baste the tops frequently as they cook.

Meanwhile, toast almonds on a baking sheet in a moderate oven for about 8-10 minutes, stirring them occasionally for even browning. Remove and allow to cool.

When pears are cooked, remove from the liquid to a serving dish. Boil the liquid to reduce it by about half. If it is still too thin to coat the pears, thicken it with 1 tbsp cornstarch dissolved in 3 tbsps water.

Pour syrup over the pears and sprinkle with almonds. Serve warm or refrigerate until lightly chilled. Garnish pears with mint leaves at the stems just before serving.

MAKES 1 PIE

PUMPKIN PIE

Pumpkins have become symbolic of our thanksgiving for autumn's harvest, and no traditional celebration would be complete without a slice of this pie!

PREPARATION TIME: 30 minutes

COOKING TIME: 50-60 minutes

PASTRY
1 cup all-purpose flour
Pinch salt
¼ cup butter, margarine or lard
Cold milk

PUMPKIN FILLING
1lb cooked and mashed pumpkin
2 eggs

1 cup evaporated milk
½ cup brown sugar
1 tsp ground cinnamon
¼ tsp ground allspice
Pinch nutmeg
Pecan halves for decoration

To prepare the pastry, sift the flour and a pinch of salt into a mixing bowl. Rub in the fat until the mixture resembles fine breadcrumbs. Stir in enough cold milk to bring the mixture together into a firm ball. Cover and chill for about 30 minutes before use.

Roll out the pastry on a lightly-floured surface to a circle about 11 inches in diameter.

Wrap the pastry around a lightly-floured rolling pin and lower it into a 10 inch round pie dish.

Press the pastry into the dish and flute the edge or crimp with a fork.

Prick the base lightly with the tines of a fork.

Combine all the filling ingredients in a mixing bowl and beat with an electric mixer until smooth. Alternatively, use a food processor. Pour into the pie crust and bake in a pre-heated 425°F oven. Bake for 10 minutes at this temperature and then lower the temperature to 350°F and bake for a further 40-50 minutes, or until the filling is set. Decorate with a circle of pecan halves.

The Yukon takes on a very different appearance during the summer months, when life is made easier without the extremities of the harsh winter weather.

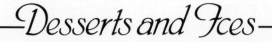

SERVES 6

FLOURLESS CHOCOLATE CAKE

This is part mousse, part soufflé, part cake and completely heavenly!
It's light but rich, and adored by chocolate lovers everywhere.

PREPARATION TIME: 20 minutes

COOKING TIME: 1 hour plus 15 minutes standing time

1lb semi-sweet chocolate	6 tbsps sugar
2 tbsps strong coffee	1 cup whipping cream
2 tbsps brandy	Powdered sugar
6 eggs	Fresh whole strawberries

Melt the chocolate in the top of a double boiler. Stir in the coffee and brandy and leave to cool slightly.

Break up the eggs and then, using an electric mixer, gradually beat in the sugar until the mixture is thick and mousse-like. When the beaters are lifted the mixture should mound slightly.

Whip the cream until soft peaks form. Beat the chocolate until smooth and shiny, and gradually add the egg mixture to it.

Fold in the cream and pour the cake mixture into a well greased 9 inch deep cake pan with a disk of wax paper in the bottom. Bake in a pre-heated 350°F oven in a bain marie. To make a bain marie, use a roasting pan and fill with warm water to come halfway up the side of the cake pan.

Bake about 1 hour and then turn off the oven, leaving the cake inside to stand for 15 minutes. Loosen the sides of the cake carefully from the pan and allow the cake to cool completely before turning it out.

Invert the cake onto a serving plate and carefully peel off the paper. Place strips of wax paper on top of the cake, leaving even spaces in between the strips. Sprinkle the top with powdered sugar and carefully lift off the paper strips to form a striped or chequerboard decoration. Decorate with whole strawberries.

Snow lightly veils the fall colors in Caledonia, Ontario.

Index